FIGHTING POVERTY & REFORMING SOCIAL SECURITY:

What Can Post-Soviet States Learn from the
New Democracies of Central Europe?

Available from the East European Studies

Woodrow Wilson International Center for Scholars
One Woodrow Wilson Plaza
1300 Pennsylvania Avenue NW
Washington, DC 20004-3027

www.wilsoncenter.org

ISBN 1-933549-15-7

**Woodrow Wilson
International
Center
for Scholars**

East European Studies

FIGHTING POVERTY AND REFORMING SOCIAL SECURITY:

What Can Post-Soviet States Learn from the New Democracies of Central Europe?

Edited by
Michael Cain,
Nida Gelazis and
Tomasz Inglot

Conference Proceedings from the meeting held
in Washington DC, June 10, 2005

The Woodrow Wilson International Center for Scholars, established by Congress in 1968 and headquartered in Washington, D.C., is a living national memorial to President Wilson. The Center's mission is to commemorate the ideals and concerns of Woodrow Wilson by providing a link between the worlds of ideas and policy, while fostering research, study, discussion, and collaboration among a broad spectrum of individuals concerned with policy and scholarship in national and international affairs. Supported by public and private funds, the Center is a nonpartisan institution engaged in the study of national and world affairs. It establishes and maintains a neutral forum for free, open, and informed dialogue. Conclusions or opinions expressed in Center publications and programs are those of the authors and speakers and do not necessarily reflect the views of the Center staff, fellows, trustees, advisory groups, or any individuals or organizations that provide financial support to the Center.

The Center is the publisher of The Wilson Quarterly and home of Woodrow Wilson Center Press, dialogue radio and television, and the monthly news-letter "Centerpoint." For more information about the Center's activities and publications, please visit us on the web at www.wilsoncenter.org.

The East European Studies (EES) program at the Woodrow Wilson International Center for Scholars provides fellowship opportunities in an effort to foster research and training on regional issues. EES offers a non-partisan forum for debate on Eastern Europe in the nation's capitol. EES organizes seminars, conferences, workshops and briefings featuring prominent scholars and policymakers. In this way, EES contributes to the aim of the Wilson Center, which is to provide a link between the world of ideas and the world of policy, bringing them into creative contact, enriching the work of both and enabling each to learn from the other.

EES contributes to the expansion of knowledge and understanding of the region by:

- bringing together prominent scholars with policy practitioners in interactive formats;
- training new generations of experts in the field;
- fostering the research work of established scholars;
- hosting an array of roundtables, conferences, policy forums, seminars and noon discussions;
- disseminating relevant policy information, in print and on the web, to a wide-ranging audience.

EAST EUROPEAN STUDIES
Woodrow Wilson International Center
for Scholars
One Woodrow Wilson Plaza
1300 Pennsylvania Avenue, NW
Washington DC 20004-3027

Tel: (202) 691-4000
Fax: (202) 691-4001

ees@wwic.si.edu
http://www.wilsoncenter.org/ees

EES STAFF
Martin C. Sletzinger, Director
Nida Gelazis, Program Associate and Editor
Jill Palmer, Program Assistant

The Kennan Institute was founded in 1974 as a division of the Woodrow Wilson International Center for Scholars through the joint initiative of Ambassador George F. Kennan, then Wilson Center Director James Billington, and historian S. Frederick Starr. Named in honor of Ambassador Kennan's relative, George Kennan "the Elder" (1845-1924), a nineteenth-century explorer of Russia and Siberia, the Kennan Institute is committed to improving American understanding of Russia, Ukraine, and other states in the region. The Institute offers residential research scholarships in the humanities and social sciences to academic scholars and specialists from government, the media, and the private sector. The Institute also administers an active program of public lectures featuring scholars and public figures, disseminating the results of its activities and research through a variety of publications. In addition, the Institute, together with Carnegie Corporation of New York, the John D. and Catherine T. MacArthur Foundation, the Ministry of Education and Science of the Russian Federation, and ISE Center (Information. Scholarship. Education.), currently administers a program supporting nine thematic social sciences and humanities research Centers for Advanced Study and Education (CASEs) established at regional Russian universities. The Kennan Institute, as part of the Wilson Center, strives to be a nexus between the world of thinkers and the world of doers, providing a neutral forum for scholarship and discussion.

The East European Studies Program presents:

Fighting Poverty and Reforming Social Security:
What Can Post-Soviet States Learn from the New Democracies of Central Europe?

Co-sponsored with St. Mary's College of Maryland
and Minnesota State University-Mankato

June 10, 2005
9:00 a.m. – 5:30 p.m.
5ᵗʰ Floor Conference Room

After decades of communist rule, reforming social policies and welfare state institutions turned out to be much more difficult and complex than previously anticipated. Regional trends emerged. Most Central European democracies introduced significant institutional reforms in social security, while changing social assistance programs to fight risks associated with poverty. In contrast, many post-Soviet states are still struggling to provide modernized and reliable welfare state protections to the elderly, the disabled and the poor during the prolonged era of political and economic transformation. This one-day conference will bring together international scholars and policy practitioners to examine patterns of welfare state development in select post-communist states and to analyze how national histories, international actors, domestic institutional contexts and the interdependence of recent social, economic and political reforms have contributed to differences in social policies and welfare state provision. Conference participants will explore major similarities and differences in social protection reform in various countries with special attention to practical and theoretical lessons of transition that can enhance our understanding of present and future problems and challenges facing the evolving post-Soviet welfare states in Russia and the neighboring states.

9:00   Registration and Coffee
9:30   Introduction: Martin Sletzinger, Director EES

9:40 Opening Remarks: Michael Cain, St. Mary's College of Maryland; **Tomasz Inglot,** Minnesota State University-Mankato

First Panel: **Tomasz Inglot,** chair

10:00 Bèla Tomka, University of Szeged, Hungary
Politics of Institutionalized Volatility: Some Lessons from East Central European Welfare Reforms

10:20 Dorottya Szikra, ELTE University, Budapest
Central and Eastern European Welfare Capitalism: The Case of the Hungarian Family and Child Support System

10:40 Andrew Konitzer, Austin College
Popular Reactions to Social and Health Sector Reforms in Russia's Regions: Reform versus Retention in Samarskaia and Ul'ianovskaia Oblasts

11:00 Discussion

**12:00 Lunch with Keynote Speaker:
Branko Milanovic,** World Bank
Poverty, Inequality and Social Policy in Postcommunist Countries: Did it All Really Matter?

Second Panel: **Michael Cain,** chair

1:30 Mitchell Orenstein, Syracuse University
Transnational Politics of Pension Reform in Kazakhstan

1:50 Janelle Kerlin, Urban Institute, Washington DC
The Politics of Decentralization and Outcomes for Social Services in Poland

2:10   **Oleksandr Rohozynsky,** CASE, Kiev, Ukraine
Increasing Social Transfers in Ukraine:
New Results and New Problems

2:30   **Discussion**

Coffee Break 3:15–3:30

Third Panel: **Robert Kaufman**, Rutgers University, chair

3:30   **Linda Cook**, Brown University
Post-Communist Welfare State Trajectories in
Eastern Europe and the Post-Soviet States

3:50   **Johan De Deken**, University of Amsterdam
Breaking the Path Dependency of Soviet Social Security:
Can Central European Experiences be Exported to the East?

4:10   **Janice Bell**, Roper Public Affairs, Washington DC
Reflections on the Polish Welfare State Reforms
in a Comparative Perspective

4:30   **Discussion**

5:15   **Summary and Closing Remarks:**
Michael Cain and **Tomasz Inglot**

CONTENTS

FROM THEORY TO PRACTICE: LESSONS OF POSTCOMMUNIST SOCIAL POLICY REFORMS IN CENTRAL EUROPE

TOMASZ INGLOT

The process of reforming or restructuring of social policies and programs in Eastern and Central Europe during the post-communist era turned out to be much longer and much more difficult than most experts anticipated. Poverty and unemployment remain widespread and persistent throughout the region. Significant changes in health care, social security and housing assistance have begun in earnest in many countries, but these projects are far from complete and, over the past decade, produced mixed results. Today, more than 15 years since the demise of the communist regimes, there are important lessons to be learned from the experiences of the so-called Central European "vanguard." Compared with countries of the former Soviet Union and those in Southeast Europe, countries such as Hungary, the Czech Republic and Poland not only made substantial progress in socio-economic and political transformation during the 1990s, but also initiated far-reaching reforms of their pension systems, unemployment insurance, health services and a variety of public assistance programs. The lessons drawn from these efforts enable us to better understand various social policy dilemmas and challenges confronted by policy makers, which have been examined by scholars, especially those currently engaged in assisting in difficult welfare state reforms in the former Soviet republics such as the Ukraine, Moldova and Kazakhstan, among others. In this introductory essay I will outline just a few general themes that explain the wider significance of the Central European experience in reforming postcommunist social policies.

In one form or another, the papers in this volume address five themes that underlie both the contemporary scholarly inquiries into postcommunist welfare states and the recent practical attempts to design and implement social policy reforms in Central and Eastern Europe and the former Soviet Union. The first theme signals a welcome change of approach within the general body of "transition literature." In fact, only since the mid-1990s have social scientists begun to seriously and systematically examine the phenomenon (and the processes) of social policy reform as a crucial dimension of postcommunist transformation; not only closely intertwined with political and economic reforms but also deserving of separate analysis on its own merits.[1] Today, few "transitologists" would argue that social policy is just a sideline issue or a simple derivative of larger and more salient economic and political change in the region. Yet, among those who study policy making and participate in welfare state restructuring in postcommunist countries, we still find a striking variety of positions. Central European policy advisers, World Bank experts and social scientists working in the region continue to express deep frustration as they witness their top concerns, priorities and warnings being passed over, ignored or outright rejected by free market ideologues, on one side, and free spending populists and defenders of the "status quo," on the other. However, as the recent pension and family policy debates in Central Europe demonstrate, on rare but important occasions social policy concerns can emerge successfully on the top of the agenda and are increasingly recognized on their own merits.[2] More detailed analysis and understanding of how and why it happens can offer important lessons for post-Soviet countries. For example, a comparison of the different dynamics and outcomes of the reform of pensions and family benefits in Poland, Hungary and the Czech Republic can show us that progress in political and economic transformation does not easily translate into similar rapid advancement in social policy. Yet, at the same time, "laggards" in the area of democratization and market reform, such as Slovakia, may become more successful in implementing important, even if highly controversial (see De Deken in this volume), social policy reforms than its more democratically advanced neighbors.

Second, as Szikra, Tomka, and De Deken and other contributors to this volume make clear, we must keep in mind that welfare state reforms involve institutional changes that affect the very core of the state structure, which is apt to prompt strong resistance. This resistance usually comes from two sources: the welfare state bureaucracies and ministries involved in policy-making and implementation, and the interested constituencies, that is, the recipients of benefits who continue to lobby the government in an attempt to preserve and/or expand the social safety net. Social security programs, in particular, represent some of the oldest and most entrenched elements of the communist-era state infrastructure throughout the region, and as such are extremely difficult to reform.[3] Due to this strong reflex to resist change, it is interesting to note that some countries, notably Poland and the Czech Republic, managed to avoid major institutional restructuring of their social security bureaucracies. Bureaucratic resilience can be explained by the fact that former communist bureaucracies face the double challenge of being simultaneously the main subjects and the main agents of reform. This situation creates tremendous pressure on the state and often undermines its already weakened capacity to effectively deliver even the existing, and admittedly inadequate, social programs, not to mention new ones recommended by domestic constituencies and international actors.

Third, many academics and policy-makers have now begun to pay much more attention to the legacies of the past and the ways in which these legacies influence meaningful change (either deterioration or improvement) and in the politics of social policy and the state capacity under democratic rule in the former communist region. It is important to keep in mind, for example, that in the late 1980s the contrast in performance and quality between the "communist welfare states" of Czechoslovakia and Albania could be no less striking when we make a similar comparison of western countries such as, for instance, Germany and Portugal in the early 1970s. Scholars[4] and policy experts[5] recognize that, before 1989, not only were communist governments poorly equipped to conduct social policy in an effective and accountable manner, but also that there were crucial differences between them. On the basis of these differences, we can now analyze with more precision significant discrepancies in the ways in which particular countries have sought to adapt their postcommunist welfare states to the conditions of democracy and free market economics since the early 1990s.

Moreover, discussions of social policy reform across the region frequently raised the crucial question of the *regime type* and the need to examine both positive and negative impacts of the consolidation of democracy on the welfare state in Central European countries. Did the introduction and practice of liberal democracy facilitate or impede welfare state reforms in Poland, Hungary, the former Czechoslovakia and perhaps other countries as well? In an attempt to answer this question, Linda Cook's contribution to this volume presents a comparative study of the post-Soviet and Central European cases. While considering the social policy development of Russia, Kazakhstan and other Central Asian states, Cook reminds us that the adoption and implementation of reforms under authoritarian conditions (in some instances perhaps even resembling the so-called "Pinochet" option in Chile of the 1980s) may have long-term consequences on these reforms. This is no less pertinent when we examine the influence of undemocratic institutions in the political sphere, but also the impact of an unreformed economic environment on the success or failure of social policy restructuring, especially in countries such as Belarus or Turkmenistan, where privatization and market liberalization have made little progress so far.

In addition, we must acknowledge that the core of consolidated democracies of Central and Eastern Europe (Poland, Hungary, Czech Republic, Slovakia, Slovenia, and the Baltic states) not only all suffer from a certain deficit of "social capital" (see Tomka in this volume) but also differ quite substantially in their approaches to "democratizing" social policy and in terms of the participation of civil society groups in the decision-making process. In fact, as De Deken notes in his contribution to this volume, all modern liberal democracies with empowered constituencies, entrenched bureaucracies and multiple veto points create powerful and often insurmountable obstacles to social policy reform. Yet, the experience of western democracies tells us that the actual extent of "welfare state retrenchment" varies greatly from one country to another.[6] In short, not only the regime type but also the model of democratic governance (now increasingly influenced by the growing body of EU law) followed can have a positive or negative impact on the quality and effectiveness of the reform process and outcome. Thus, as we engage in this type of institutional analysis of the politics of social policy, we need to recognize the full complexity of this endeavor. In particular, we need to carefully distinguish which lessons of social policy reform are useful and applicable across different postcommunist regimes, and which apply exclusively to a narrow group of more or less consolidated democracies of Central Europe.

Fourth, the fate of many necessary social policy reforms that were introduced before the mid-1990s to a large extent depended on a government's ability to forge consensus around some kind of positive vision regarding the specific type of welfare state that would be socially and politically acceptable, but also economically feasible. Sometimes, this emerging consensus, or the lack thereof, can be traced back to ideological shifts and the dynamics of party politics of the early transition period.[7] But it is also heavily grounded in the more distant past, reflecting not just a legacy of communist (Marxist-Leninist) rule[8] but also an elaborate mixture of national, conservative, socialist and liberal, influences throughout political histories of various countries.[9]

In many cases—at least at the beginning of the reform process in the early 1990s—the debate over the appropriate ideological foundation of social policy or desired welfare state model was framed very much in a negative way. It was often driven by populist sentiments that could be summed up in a simple statement: "keep your welfare promises better than the communists did, but don't take away any benefits." As Tomka points out in this volume, despite widely hailed progress in democratic consolidation, civil societies in Central Europe remain rather weak and disengaged, especially when it comes to active participation in shaping the welfare state. Serious debates over the most appropriate welfare models have taken place mostly at the elite level. Initially, many policy makers and advisors expressed a rather utopian belief in being able to create an Austrian-style or German-style social market economy, or even a Scandinavian kind of a social-democratic welfare state. On the other side of the ideological divide, however, a smaller but vocal minority of politicians and experts, mostly economists, advocated an American type of a "residual" model with limited state involvement. Rather uncritically, they championed this model as a necessary antidote to an "overprotective" communist welfare state (see Szikra and De Deken in this volume).

Despite this fervent clash of foreign-inspired welfare ideologies, since the mid-1990s many Central European countries have begun to develop their own visions of the welfare state based more soundly on domestic experiences and traditions, although not completely free from outside assistance and inspiration. Today, by critically examining how successful these efforts have been in Central Europe we could discover a great deal more about the possibility of creating a stable, pro-welfare consensus in various parts of the postcommunist region. For example, the Czechs have long claimed to have forged some type of a "socio-liberal" consensus, based on relatively generous social spending. Hungarians seem to have reached a tentative agreement on a leaner welfare state based more on cash transfers and less on social services, with better targeted social assistance that could potentially lower the tax burden on employers. Drawing on these and other useful experiences from Central Europe, we can investigate whether or not a similar phenomenon of "nationalizing" the postcommunist welfare state could take place in Russia and other post-Soviet states and study the ways in which a new societal consensus, even if originating "from above," can help produce more effective social policies.

Finally, the fifth theme deals more directly with practical problems of policy-making and implementation. It underscores the importance of examining and identifying a clear hierarchy of need in each post-communist society and, more specifically, the distinct needs of a certain locality (see Konitzer in this volume). Precise targeting of various social groups for the delivery of distinct forms of government assistance at different levels, often combined with decentralizing administrative reforms (see Kerlin in this volume) has long been supported by the international organizations involved in the region, such as the World Bank and USAID. Indeed, Central European governments, which have accumulated valuable experience in fighting poverty among the elderly, for example, could offer useful help and expertise in this area to the former Soviet republics.[10] As many contributors to this volume show, real progress in the area of benefit targeting has been painfully slow. Yet, I would argue that more attention to these efforts, especially ones conducted increasingly at the subnational level, is absolutely necessary to grasp the complexity of income protection and the often unexpected ways in which countries can learn from each other how to better safeguard their populations against the negative effects of the prolonged and still highly unpredictable process of socioeconomic transformation. As contributors to this conference have showed, many of these reforms have been conducted on a trial and error basis. Although this is understandable given the constantly changing socioeconomic context (including the emergence of new types and concentrations of poverty within different countries), a growing number of observers believe that western nations bear a large share of the blame for offering poor advice and misusing financial assistance to postcommunist countries.

This question again touches on one of the leading themes of the conference, namely the crucial issue of the interdependence of political, economic and social policy reforms. Which Central European countries have been the most successful in combining the major goals of all of these spheres, and what we can learn from this experience? Both case studies and comparative analyses of these countries can offer a highly illuminating mix of answers to this important question, especially when we attempt to assess changes in specific program areas, such as family benefits or pensions in more detail (see Szikra and Orenstein in this volume). In addition, we can look at the Polish experience with social transfers to miners and collective farmers, the Czechoslovak experience with price subsidies from the early 1990s, the Slovak experience with the programs directed to the most impoverished groups, such as the Roma, and a whole spectrum of innovations and experiments with unemployment programs across Central Europe in the broad context of the post-1989 transformation.

I realize that in my short introduction I was barely able to scratch the surface of this extremely broad area of investigation. As De Deken reminds us in his critical essay in this volume, we should be fully aware that there are certain definitive barriers to what reform ideas, policy prescriptions or practical experiences can really be successfully transferred, whether from West to East or within the family of the former communist countries. Still, all participants in this conference seem to agree that we need to do much more to explore such possibilities and continue the long-term effort to draw valuable lessons from the ongoing transformations of the welfare state in postcommunist Europe.

ENDNOTES

1 Ethan B Kapstein and Michael Mandelbaum, *Sustaining the Transition: The Social Safety Net in Postcommunist Europe* (New York: The Council on Foreign Relations, 1997), Linda Cook, Mitchell A. Orenstein, and Marilyn Rueschemeyer, eds., *Left Parties and Social Policy in Postcommunist Europe.* (Boulder CO: Westview Press, 1999), and Katharina Müller, *The Political Economy of Pension Reform in Central-Eastern Europe.* (Cheltenham, UK/Northampton, MA: Edward Elgar, 1999).

2 Elaine Fultz, ed., *Pension Reform in Central and Eastern Europe,: Restructuring with Privatization: Case Studies of Hungary and Poland* (vol.1) and *Restructuring of Public Pension Schemes: Case Studies of the Czech Republic and Slovenia* (vol.2) (Budapest: International Labour Organization, 2002) and Tomasz Inglot,

"Historical Legacies, Institutions and the Politics of Social Policy in Hungary and Poland, 1989-1999," In Grzegorz Ekiert and Stephen Hanson, eds., *Capitalism and Democracy in Eastern and Central Europe: Assessing the Legacy of Communist Rule* (New York: Cambridge University Press, 2003). See also Orenstein and Szikra in this volume.

3. Agnieszka Chloń–Domińczak, "The Polish Pension Reform of 1999." In Fultz, *Pension Reform* (vol.1), 95-205, Inglot, "Historical Legacies," and also see Andrea Chandler, *Shocking Mother Russia: Democratization, Social Rights, and Pension Reform in Russia, 1990-2001* (Toronto: Toronto University Press, 2004).

4. Kapstein and Mandelbaum, *Sustaining the Transition*, Inglot, "Historical Legacies," Chandler, *Shocking Mother Russia*, and Bela Tomka, *Welfare in East and West:* Hungarian Social Security in an International Comparison (Berlin: Akademie Verlag, 2004). See also Tomka in this volume.

5. Fultz, *Pension Reform* (vols.1and 2), and Nicholas Barr, ed., *Labor Markets and Social Policy in Central and Eastern Europe: The Accession and Beyond* (Washington DC: World Bank, 2005).

6. Paul Pierson, *Dismantling the Welfare State? Reagan, Thatcher, and the Politics of Retrenchment* (New York: Cambridge University Press, 1994) and Giuliano Bonoli, *The Politics of Pension Reform: Institutions and Policy Change in Western Europe.* (Cambridge, UK: Cambridge University Press, 2000).

7. Cook, Orenstein, Rueschemeyer, *Left Parties and Social Policy.*

8. Claus Offe, "The Politics of Social Policy in East European Transitions," *Social Research* 4 (Winter 1993): 639-684 and James R Millar and Sharon L. Wolchik, eds., *The Social Legacy of Communism* (New York and Washington DC: Cambridge University Press/Woodrow Wilson Center Press, 1994).

9. Johan Jeroen De Deken, "Social Policy in Postwar Czechoslovakia. The Development of Old-Age Pensions and Housing Policies during the Period 1945-1989," *EUI Working Paper SPS.* 94/13 (1994) (Florence: European University Institute) and David Stark and Laszlo Bruszt, *Postsocialist Pathways: Transforming Politics and Property in East Central Europe* (New York: Cambridge University Press, 1998), Inglot, "Historical Legacies," and Tomka, *Welfare in East and West.*

10. See for example Robert Holzman and Richard Hinz, *Old Age Income Support in the 21ˢᵗ Century. An International Perspective on Pension Systems and Reform* (Washington DC: The World Bank, 2005).

BREAKING THE PATH DEPENDENCY OF SOVIET SOCIAL SECURITY: CAN CENTRAL EUROPEAN EXPERIENCES BE EXPORTED TOWARDS THE EAST?

Johan J. De Deken

Two ideas seem to be central to a discussion on postcommunist welfare reform: on the one hand, there is the idea of policy learning, that is, the assumption that the countries that arose out of the debris of the Soviet Union (to which I will refer as CIS countries) can draw practical and theoretical lessons from the reforms that were implemented or are in the process of being implemented in the new democracies of Central and Eastern Europe (which in this paper I call NDCE countries). On the other hand, there is the idea of path dependency, that is, that all post-soviet societies have something in common when it comes to the prospects of reforming their social security, health care and income support systems. In this chapter, I will discuss the limits of both of these ideas, arguing that even though technically it would not have been that difficult to modernize the social security systems that Eastern Europe inherited from the Soviet period, by adopting a series of incremental reforms, most governments embarked upon a Schumpeterian project of "creative destruction"—throwing out the baby with the bath water. Rather then implementing parametrical reforms to rectify some of the problems that marred the old system or that came to the forefront with the transition from a command to market economy (such as the low contribution moral or the lack of an adequate indexation mechanism), the very essentials of encompassing collectively-financed welfare arrangements were put into question. In countries where democracy has made more headway, this neo-liberal reform project may have had to be disguised by a so-called "tactical sequencing" or by the temporary introduction of hybrid models in order to gain support. The ultimate aim, though, seems to have been the same, namely to accomplish as much as possible a return to the "night watchman state" of the 19th century.

Postcommunist reformers appear to have learned precious little from the policy practices in Western welfare states. This lack of learning was observable first in the NDCE countries in their relation to Western experiences, and now seems to be repeated by the CIS countries, both in relation to what happened in the West, as well as in relation to the more recent developments in NDCE countries. Most policy makers in the region seem to be stirred by an ideological zeal that echoes Soviet times, although the ideology is no longer Marxist-Leninist, but possessive liberalism. If in Soviet times social policy was used to advance industrialization, it is now completely subordinated to the goal of establishing a market economy. One of the most lasting legacies of the Soviet era seems to be the discrediting of most forms of state intervention in general, and of the ideals of equality and social solidarity in particular. Unreformed communists have joined forces with populists and nationalists in rhetorically expropriating the very idea of social protection and solidarity, making a democratic representation of these interests difficult, if not impossible. The appeal of individualized, visible ownership claims combined with a general lack of understanding of the negative long-term effects of a market economy without an adequate social insurance system seem to have made it possible for these countries to radically break with their communist past, even if the political conditions that made this rupture possible are part of that very same legacy. In the end, the losers of the neo-liberal transformation may further push the hand of nationalist and populist charlatans, thereby placing these fragile democracies further into jeopardy.

One could argue that some tactical lessons from the Western countries have been drawn by governments in NDCE countries, and in CIS countries from both the West and from NDCE countries. But they copied short-term ploys that would help them get away with policies that will increase inequality and poverty in the long-term, rather than help to fight it. The traumatic experience of Soviet communism, combined with their weak position within the international political economy and their structural indebtedness, made postcommunist countries susceptible to the radical neoliberal recipes prescribed by the knowledge brokers in international organizations (such as the World Bank) who could back up their advice with generous aid packages and structural loans.

THE LIMITS OF POLICY LEARNING

Over the past decade, there has been a renewed interest in the idea of policy learning in the analysis of social policy reform. Policy learning, which involves importing social policy models from other contexts, can be traced back to the very origins of the welfare state.[1] But what is new is the optimism expressed by an increasing number of academics and social policy makers. For example, the European Commission has sought to promote the so-called Open Method of Coordination (OMC), which accomplished some minor successes in the field of labor market policies and social inclusion, though it has had limited impact on pension and health care reform. This is partly due to the fact that for these latter fields it turned out to be too difficult for the countries involved to come to an agreement on the goals of the reforms. To some extent, these disagreements arose from the different economic and political conditions of these countries. This contextual incompatibility makes policy learning problematic.

Such differences in economic development and political environment are even more evident between CIS states that want to learn from NDCE countries. In the contribution of Dorittya Szikra in this volume, for example, one can see that the debates of population policy, such as boosting fertility, play a central part in Hungary's social policies. Yet, because the issue is not important in Poland, and even less so in a country such as Kazakhstan, policy learning from the Hungarian example would not be appropriate for Poland or Kazakhstan.

Given this limitation, one wonders what is the basis of the optimism shared by advocates of policy learning as a governance mechanism? It is debatable to what extent national policy elites (or the bulk of their electorate, for that matter) will go along in adopting policies that are radically different from those that prevail in their own country.[2] One can question how much foreign examples can really help to break the bounded rationality of policy makers, who want to avoid the costs associated with a pure trial-and-error learning.[3]

To a limited extent, policy learning might be feasible at the level of abstract ideas and general policy concepts. But at the level of implementing concrete policies and of reforming real institutions, 'learned' policies are likely to (1) meet considerable political resistance by the affected interest groups or (2) face the problem that reform blueprints are incompatible with existing institutions. The first problem has been discussed at length in the literature regarding so-called "veto players" and "veto points," as demonstrated in this volume by Linda Cook's account of the stagnation of the reform process in the Russian Federation and of the divergent reform paths taken by Kazakhstan and Belarus. The second problem builds upon the idea of institutional complementarities advanced by the varieties of capitalism approach.[4] It implies that even if one expects learning and mutual adjustment to occur across policy elites, the identification of a "best practice" in other countries does not necessarily point to an appropriate strategy by which this practice can be adapted to a different institutional context. Thus, it is possible to identify three situations in which policy transfers fail to accomplish their intended effect:[5]

1. an *uninformed* transfer: the borrowing country may lack sufficient information about the policy, in particular about the way it operates in the country from which it is borrowed;
2. an *incomplete* transfer: crucial elements of what made a policy or an institutional arrangement a success in one country are left out in the transfer;
3. an *inappropriate* transfer: in adopting policies from other countries, policy makers may pay insufficient attention to the different economic, social or ideological context of the borrowing country.

The OMC in the European Union, as well as various comparative studies on the reform process in NDCE countries (including this volume), seek to contribute to a solution to the first type of failure. The second type of failure is all too often the result of eager policy makers or policy advisers that selectively use foreign examples in support of their ideological project, thus also deliberately or inadvertently committing the third type of failure. Moreover, the policy learning paradigm also seems to underestimate the power inequalities in the international learning community. Learning is not a neutral process. Competing policy entrepreneurs, advocacy coalitions and lobbyists "sell" policies and they use the resources available to them while pursuing their goals. For example, the World Bank had much more influence "advising" on pension and labor market reforms than the International Labor Organization, simply because it could back up this "advice" with generous technical assistance and transition loans (see Orenstein in this volume).

WHAT IS PATH DEPENDENCY?

Central to the idea of path dependency is the assumption that once a country has started down one policy track, the costs of reversal are very high.[6] Perhaps the metaphor of a tree more closely resembles this dynamic, as most proponents of this approach recognize that starting from similar conditions—or one tree trunk—a wide range of outcomes—or branches—may be possible, and that important consequences may result from relatively small contingent events.[7] Some branches die (as seems to have been the case with almost all former Soviet regimes in Central Eastern Europe), and countries can try to jump from one branch to another (which seems to be the predominant pattern throughout the region).

In the context of Western Europe, the notion of path dependency has often been invoked to explain the lack of radical reforms or drastic welfare state retrenchment.[8] The prototype for this trend was the resilience of the British National Health Service to Margaret Thatcher's attempts to radically privatize it. This resilience is often explained by invoking a rather narrow concept of path dependency, which emphasizes self-reinforcing positive feedback processes and so-called "increasing returns," which means that over time the costs of exiting from one path and entering another tend to rise.[9] This is due to high set-up costs, which include the accumulation of expertise, coordination effects and the effects of the vested interests of various constituencies, which tend to build up over time. Therefore, one of the reasons that the Czech Republic was, compared to other NDCE countries, less receptive to foreign advice was the existence of a vast stock of local knowledge and expertise that existed in the country.

THE COMMON TRUNK OF THE SOVIET ERA

The common "tree trunk," from which East European countries developed their own welfare paths, consists of the legacy of Soviet-style social insurance, an extensive system of price subsidies in areas such as rent, energy and food, and various enterprise-based fringe benefits, such as access to health care, leisure facilities and housing. I will discuss this legacy by focusing primarily on the old-age pension insurance system that was in force in Czechoslovakia. After a series of reforms in the 1950s, all East European countries ended up with a unified system that was integrated into the state budget, thereby allowing for cross-subsidizing other expenditure items.[10] Employees' contributions were largely abolished, but benefits remained earnings-related and on the number of years worked. The problem, though, is that only countries that already had an experienced welfare administration (inherited from their "Bismarckian" pre-war system) were actually keeping records of individual earnings. It was only in those countries that the system was technically truly earnings-related.[11]

The stratifying impact of the earnings-related nature of these universal schemes was far less than in capitalist market economies, since wage differentials were limited (Czechoslovakia probably had the most compressed wage structure in the entire developed world), full employment was more or less guaranteed, and labor force participation rates (up to the statutory retirement age) were extremely high for both men and women. This de facto full employment that existed meant that people were able to keep their jobs even if they did not perform well. As a consequence, there was far less benefit differentiation in the social security systems of Eastern Europe than in earnings related systems in Western countries.

The most important inequalities were a consequence of a series of privileges granted to those who were employed in occupations that were considered of strategic importance. Those groups benefited from more advantageous benefit formulas. This principle of favoring certain occupations that were considered central to the model of draft industrialization was applied in other important social policy areas such as housing.

To the extent that East European social insurance was Bismarckian, this can hardly be considered a legacy of the interwar period, but rather should be seen as inherent to the Soviet project of transforming society. Soviet communists implemented something that was much closer to what Bismarck originally had in mind, than those systems that are now called the Bismarckian.[12] Béla Tomka, in his contribution to this volume, has made a similar qualification of the apparent Bismarckian precedents of the systems in Central and Eastern Europe. The formal earnings-related nature of postwar social security systems in Eastern Europe was not so much the consequence of a policy legacy of the interwar period, but rather can be related to the imposition of a Stalinist model of draft industrialization. Thus the centrality of work, or the similarities to what Richard Titmuss called the "work performance model," can be traced down to a Marxist-Leninist ideology that sought to reward industrial production and labor force mobilization.[13]

Moreover, Bismarck originally wanted to impose central state control, but opposition to his plans forced him to introduce the type of autonomous corporatist social insurance schemes that are currently referred to as Bismarckian. In Soviet countries, we see a closer embodiment of Bismarck's original ideas in force, since even if unions had formal responsibilities in the administration of social insurance, it was de facto a state controlled system. Soviet communists used central state control for the very same Bonapartist reasons Bismarck originally had preferred this method of administration: they hoped that state paternalism would encourage loyalty and dependence vis-à-vis the Soviet state.

The other main source of inequality in Soviet Eastern Europe was the insufficient indexation of pension benefits to price or wage dynamics. This stemmed from the ideological imperative that the Soviet system would make inflation impossible—indeed, the official line was that consumer prices would decline over time. This design deficiency had particularly important ramifications in those countries that traditionally suffered from inflation, such as Poland. As a consequence, newly granted benefits were considerably higher than average benefits. It was this problem of the so-called "old age portfolio" that arguably became one of the biggest problems once prices began to soar with the transformation of the economy after 1989.

Thus, the legacy of soviet social insurance consisted of a centralized, pay-as-you-go system that was remarkably close to what Otto von Bismarck originally had in mind. The schemes were earnings-related and offered de facto universal coverage, but lacked the proper indexation of benefits. Formally, they were administered by the trade unions, but these simply operated as transmission belts of the communist controlled state apparatus. In other segments of the welfare state, most notably health care, Soviet countries more closely resembled a social democratic model of a national health service (even if in comparison to Scandinavian countries health care in some countries was more centralized, while in others some of the health care facilities were linked to factories and thus varied with the economic importance of a region).[14]

Finally, the legacy of communism also meant that important pillars of the Western welfare state were missing. In particular, unemployment insurance schemes and a system of means-tested poverty relief did not exist:[15] either people were employed in non-productive jobs, or they received an old-age or disability pension. The only other alternatives were various forms of maternity leave or maternity benefits (for the Hungarian case, see the Dorottya Szikra in this volume).

Given the nature of soviet economies, cash transfers in general played a far less important role in social policy regimes. Decommodification was, in contrast to most West European welfare states, not primarily realized by an extensive income transfer system, but rather by administrating the market at the level of the production of goods and services. Basic goods and services, ranging from housing, energy and food to transport, health care and child care, were often provided for well below their true costs. Guy Standing therefore convincingly has argued that soviet communism left behind a "service heavy, transfer light" social policy regime.[16]

WHAT COULD HAVE BEEN DONE GIVEN THIS LEGACY?

In principle, this legacy ought to have made possible a relatively smooth transformation from the soviet social security model to a sort of conservative-corporatist model of social insurance: one only needed to implement a number of parametric reforms:

(1) the reintroduction of a closer link between benefits and lifetime earnings, not only by individualizing benefits (as had been the case in a number of soviet countries), but also individualizing contributions (making the earnings-related benefit again more conditional upon an actual record of payment of contributions);[17]

(2) the introduction of social assistance and unemployment insurance;

(3) the reintroduction of parity financing (to replace the exclusive reliance upon employer contributions) and the inclusion of

employer representatives on the administration boards (in order to improve the control and accountability of these organs);

(4)   the development of an adequate benefit indexation mechanism.

Within the environment of a capitalist market economy, a reformed Bismarckian earnings-related social insurance would also have led to an increase in income inequality. But because of the inclusive character of such a scheme, it would also have kept such rising inequality under control, just as has been the case in the social market economies of post-war continental Europe.

The reform of welfare services was bound to be more problematic, given their partial intertwinement with the large, defunct industrial conglomerates. While in many of the NDCEs health care did not need a complete overhaul, in those countries in which health care was linked to factories, the wave of bankruptcies that followed privatization meant a considerable share of welfare provision disappeared overnight, and had to be replaced by a genuine form of public provision (such enterprise-based health care seemed to have been more prevalent in CIS countries than in NDCE countries). In the area of health care the most pressing problem throughout Eastern Europe was corruption (see Béla Tomka in this volume). With the collapse of Communist Party discipline, this type of corruption has become even more widespread during the transition years.

WHAT WAS DONE SINCE 1989?

Once they embarked upon reforming their social security systems, most countries in Eastern Europe went much further than the kinds of parametrical reforms I describe above. Some observers have come to the conclusion that what actually happened was the initiation of a neo-liberal welfare state model (or a "residual welfare state" as Richard Titmuss described it). When soviet communism collapsed, the baby seems to have been thrown out with the bath water. No attempt was made to introduce genuine corporatist self-government of social insurance or to democratize public welfare provision. Rather than moving towards a hybrid of a continental social market economy and Scandinavian type public welfare provision that would have kept "'Western' features of the social system and throwing away 'Eastern'-type pseudo paternalism," the essentials of collectively-financed and publicly-provided welfare arrangements were put into question.[18]

For example, if one considers pension reforms, the only two countries that evolved closer to the West European continental model of social insurance, were Slovenia and the Czech Republic. Other countries adopted hybrid models with so-called "opt-out" clauses, which over time are bound to evolve into a type of welfare state that is even more privatized than what currently exists in many Western countries that approximate Esping-Andersen's liberal world of welfare capitalism.[19] The prime model for pension reforms in Eastern Europe seems to have been Latin America, and in particular Chile, rather than any of the three worlds of welfare capitalism in the OECD area.

However, even if some countries, in particular Kazakhstan, seem to have attempted to outstrip the best pupil of the World Bank school—Pinochet's Chile—most countries so far seem to have been more cautious and have implemented a watered down version of this neo-liberal model. The less a country has democratized, the more it seems likely to adhere to some orthodoxy, whether it be to the old soviet orthodoxy (as is the case in Belarus) or to the new neo-liberal orthodoxy advocated by the World Bank (as is evident in Kazakhstan). In the former case, the executive power seems to rely on the inherited state and administrative structures, while in the later, the authoritarian state allied itself with oligarchs, who favor economic liberalization (see the contributions by Linda Cook, Andrew Konitzer and Mitchell Orenstein in this volume). The more a country had to contend with a well organized opposition with veto powers, the more they seem to have been forced into compromise, resulting in a hybrid reforms, the success of which is still unclear (see Béla Tomka and Dorottya Szikra in this volume).

The irony in all this is that, just as the 1950s-era Marxist-Leninist vanguard of Stalinists instrumentalized the reform of (or, in some countries, introduced) the social security system to foster draft industrialization, the 1990s neo-liberals sought to instrumentalize reforms of social security to promote their market liberal reforms. In both cases "social policy reforms" in the end had very little to do with the goal of setting up a well-functioning system of social security or combating poverty. Just as the Stalinists of the 1950s saw draft industrialization as a precondition for economic growth and aggregate wealth, so do neo-liberal reformers today consider a completely free market as a guarantor for a economic growth and an aggregate prosperity that will automatically solve the poverty problem. In neither of these two worldviews does there seem to be a place for social security as an autonomous policy instrument to combat poverty and inequality.

In terms of health care and social services, in most postcommunist countries we witnessed a retreat from previous levels of state provision, with private non-profit and for-profit initiatives only haphazardly filling in the gaps. Most non-governmental welfare organizations turned out to have a low capacity for delivering public goods, or offered rather mediocre quality of care and services. They tend to favor the rich and are often set up to serve nefarious purposes, namely tax evasion.[20] Private health and pension insurance have been less efficient both in terms of coverage and benefit security, and have much more administrative overhead than publicly administered schemes. In this respect they are not any different from their counterparts in the Western Europe and North America. But given the immaturity of the new markets, and in view of the fact that problems such as missing markets, adverse selection and information asymmetries are even more problematic in Eastern Europe than they are in the West, the waste of valuable resources is probably even higher, which means that private provision is an even more a risky strategy that is bound to aggravate high social inequality and poverty.

Eastern Europe lacks the institutions necessary socially embedding its new markets. Third party problems, lack of payment morale and moral hazard can be expected to form even more of a problem given the institutional legacy of corruption and social distrust. Often, the lack of professionalism and widespread corruption in East European bureaucracies is invoked to justify a far-reaching privatization.[21] But if a government is ineffective, any social security system will be at risk, whether private or public.[22] Rather than automatically opting for privatization, countries in this region should petition for international support to develop good public governance.

Finally, it should be recognized that the emergence of hybrid forms reflects a drastic break from the institutional past and gives us reason to cast doubt on the usual path dependency arguments: after all, they involve quite drastic retrenchment policies. Irrespective of their political colors or of the will of the population, most governments in Central and Eastern Europe have been able to embark upon implementing quite far-reaching neo-liberal reforms.

SO WHY SO MUCH RETRENCHMENT?

How, then, can we account for the fact that East European governments got away with such radical retrenchment policies? One reason could be related to the fact that soviet communism had quite a devastating effect in discrediting state intervention in general and the ideals of equality and solidarity in particular.[23] Political parties and other social actors (such as the largely discredited trade unions) that might have represented the welfare interests of the population have been notoriously weak. Moreover, the free market transition and the huge development gap that needed to be bridged between East and West Europe meant that proponents of welfare issues felt blackmailed into submission by threats that welfare benefits would lead to further unemployment, or by accusations of being conspirators of the ancient regime. A coalition of nationalists and unreformed communists continues to rhetorically expropriate the idea of social protection and solidarity, preventing an effective and democratic organization of welfare interests in most countries.

At the same time, it has been argued that privatization of social security does appeal to individualized, visible ownership claims,[24] especially in such areas as pensions, where the potential risks of private provision and the transition costs of introducing a new system are not transparent. The impact of these measures may only be felt in the next few decades. By that time, it will be too late to reverse the policies that are now initiated: apparently limited reforms in place now may end up having large lasting consequences in the future.

Neo-liberal reforms were also strongly supported by international organizations, which not only operated as 'knowledge brokers,' but also handed out structural adjustment loans to back their neo-liberal reform agendas. For example, the World Bank granted Kazakhstan a $300 million loan to finance its transition from a public pay-as-you-go to a fully funded private pension scheme.[25] A few years earlier, the Bank approved a $150 million "Public Sector Adjustment Loan" in order to support the partial privatization of the Hungarian pension system. Only countries with relatively low indebtedness, such as the Czech Republic, seem to have been able to resist the pressure and temptation from the Bank.[26] And even if reforms in countries such as Poland and Hungary ended up being a far cry from the radical Chilean pension model, they still have had considerable secondary effects: "as contributions will be increasingly drained away from the public system, it has a built-in mechanism towards shrinking the PAYG tier, making the public scheme even ore unsustainable, fiscally as well as politically."[27] The very purpose of partial privatization seems to have been to strengthen constituent support in favor of more radical reforms and to weaken veto actors. From the point of view of radical reformers, the current compromise is no more than an intermediate stage that gradually will be phased out. In this context, the World Bank has recommended a "tactical sequencing" that is to allow participants to opt out of a public scheme in order to be able to phase them out at a later stage.[28]

Such a strategy had already been pursued with considerable success (that is from the neo-liberal reformers point of view) in the UK when the Thatcher governments introduced the possibility to "opt out" of SERPS, which led to a gradual erosion of the public earnings related scheme. Another example of tactical sequencing was the attempt to co-opt some of the veto players. Again, Hungary offers a good example. The Hungarian government decided to set up the pension funds as non-profit mutual benefit associations formally controlled by the members and the trade unions. De facto, however it is often outside for-profit enterprises that collect contributions, administer and invest the funds, and pay annuities.[29]

The extent of retrenchment seems also to be related to the strength of the Ministries of Welfare vis-à-vis the Ministries of Finance, and on how much expert knowledge on social security existed within the country. It therefore should not come as surprise that one of the countries that pioneered social insurance, the Czech Republic, was the most resilient against the lure of adopting the World Bank's prescriptions. By contrast, Kazakhstan is at the opposite end of the spectrum, as is the other successor state of Czechoslovakia—Slovakia—given the recent wave of neo-liberal reforms adopted there and the paucity of domestic social security experts.

Conclusion

If one looks at the social reform processes in Eastern Europe, one might indeed witness policy learning by the NDCE from the West, and by the CIS from both NDCE and from the West, which would allow those countries to break the path dependency of the soviet social security system. However, one must question whether the right lessons have been applied. Most of the learning seems to have been a sort of mimicking marred by all the three types of policy transfer traps, of which Dolowitz and Marsh warned us.

In the area of pensions and health care reform, we find uninformed transfers based on the myth that private provision is more efficient and cost effective than public provision. What makes things even worse is that the deficiencies of private forms of provision, such as missing markets and information asymmetries, are even more likely to occur in postcommunist countries, because they lack the Durkheimian "non-contractual elements of a contract" necessary for such arrangements to offer some security. Similarly, one could argue that in CIS countries, enterprise-based welfare is more suitable and therefore should not be dismantled. In contrast to NDCE countries, CIS countries cannot, in the foreseeable future, hope for integration into West European markets via membership in the European Union. Therefore, what might have been a sensible strategy in the former countries might not work in the latter.

An example of an incomplete transfer is the introduction of flexible deregulated labor markets without simultaneously setting up an adequate unemployment system and the kind of basic old age pension guarantees that even most Bismarckian welfare states in Western Europe have.

Finally, an example of an inappropriate transfer is the attempt to create a neo-liberal welfare state without a strong affluent economy, and thus the high average standard of living that is required to justify a weak welfare state. Also lacking in postcommunist Europe is the charitable tradition of Anglo-American liberal welfare states, as well as the strong family ties that typically accompany Southern European "latin rim" welfare states.

If one wants to assess the (potential) successes of a reform, it is important to distinguish two different purposes that the reform can serve. If the end aim is to unburden the state as much as possible from responsibilities, and to create a night watchman state, some of the reform measures such as hybrid welfare state with opt-out clauses and tactical sequencing, might be considered the recipes for success. Such measures indeed might diffuse popular opposition to a great neo-liberal transformation of society in the short term.

If, by contrast, the aim of the reforms is to create a sustainable and adequate system of social security to compensate for the rising inequalities that come with the introduction of a capitalist market economy, the path followed by most NDCE countries (which is now mimicked or even radicalized in some CIS states) is not to be recommend, because it will end up dramatically increasing inequality and poverty in the region. In the longer term, such inequalities may strengthen populist or even authoritarian movements, which may not only challenge the short-term tactical success of the neo-liberal project, but also could end up putting at risk the still fragile foundations of the new democracies in the region.

ENDNOTES

1. Thus in the first decade of the 20th century British politicians such as Llyoyd George visited Germany to study its welfare arrangements. In some areas this led to the adoption of the German model (for example the Labor exchange Act of 1908). In other areas, however, the British did not copy the German model (for example the National Insurance Act of 1911)

2. For a discussion of this kind of "greater opportunities" argument, see Zeitlin, Jonathan "Introduction" in Jonathan Zeitlin & David Trubeck, eds. Governing Work and Welfare in a New Economy Oxford: Oxford University Press, (2003) pp.1-30.

3. As is for instance suggested by Dutch Central Planning Office, "Challenging Neighbours. Rethinking German and Dutch Economic Institutions" Den Haag: Centraal Planbureau 1997.

4. Hall, Peter A. Hall & Soskice, David eds. Varieties of Capitalism. The Institutional Foundations of Comparative Advantage Oxford, UK: Oxford University Press, (2001) pp.1-68.

5. Dolowitz, David P. & Marsh, David "Learning from Abroad: The Role of Policy Transfer in Contemporary Policy Making" in Governance: An International Journal of Policy and Administration Vol.13, No.1, (2000) pp.5-24.

6. Levi, Margaret "A Model, a Method, and a Map: Rational Choice in Comparative Historical Analysis" in Mark I. Lichbach & Alan S, Zuckerman Comparative Politics: Rationality, Culture, and Structure Cambridge: Cambridge University Press, (1997) pp.19-41.

7. Pierson, Paul "Increasing Returns, Path Dependency, and the Study of Politics" in American Political Science Review Vol.94, No.2, (2000) pp.251-267.

8. Pierson, Paul "Irresistible Forces, Immovable Objects: Post-Industrial Welfare States Confront Permanent Austerity" in Journal of European Public Policy Vol.5, No.4, (1998) pp.539-60.

9. op.cit 7.

10. Muller, Katharina "Beyond privatization: pension reform in the Czech Republic and Slovenia" in Journal of European Social Policy Vol.12, No.4, (2002) pp. 293-306.

11. Kathrina Müller claims that this was the exception, and that only "few CEE and FSU countries kept individual contribution records prior to 1989". May-be only countries with a strong prewar social insurance tradition (basically those countries that developed from the debris of the Austro-Hungarian empire) might have continued keeping track of earnings. Müller, Katharina "From the State to the Market? Pension Reform Paths in Central-Eastern Europe and the Former Soviet Union" in Social Policy and Administration Vol.36, No.2, (2003) pp.156-175.

12. Rimlinger, Gaston V. Welfare Policy and Industrialization in Europe, America and Russia New York, NY: John Wiley (1971).

13. Titmuss, Richard M. "Policy. An Introduction" London: Allen & Unwin (1974).

14. In some countries (such as Czechoslovakia), this concerned only child care facilities and holiday homes (in Slovak part on the country, only the East Slovak Steel Works VSŽ had – and still has – its own hospital), in other countries (such as the Soviet Union) the importance of enterprise-based welfare seems to have been much more important.

15. Thus, in Czechoslovakia the only forms of social assistance that existed were benefits targeted at children, and at the elderly (the so-called social pensions).

16. Standing, Guy "Social Protection in Central and Eastern Europe. A Tale of Slippery Anchors and Torn Safety Nets" in Gøsta Esping-Andersen, ed. Welfare States in Transition. National Adaptations in Global Economies London: Sage, (1996) pp.225-255.

17. Futz, Elaine & Stanovnik, Tine "The Collection of Pension Contributions: Trends, Issues and Problems in Central and Eastern Europe" Budapest: International Labor Office (2004).

18. Kovács, János Mátyás "Approaching the EU and Reaching the US? Rival Narratives on Transforming Welfare Regimes in East-Central Europe" in *Western European Politics* Vol.25, No.2, (2002) pp.175-204.

19. Esping-Andersen, Gøsta "The Three Worlds of Welfare Capitalism" Princeton, NJ: Princeton University Press (1990).

20. op. cit. 18

21. Kornai, János "Reform of the Welfare Sector in Post Communist Countries: A Normative Approach" in Joan M. Nelson, et al eds. Transforming

Post-Communist Political Economies Washington DC: National Academy Press, (1997) pp.276-298.

22. Barr, Nicholas "Reforming Pensions: Myths, Truths and Policy Choices" in Reforming Public Pensions. Sharing the Experience of Transition and OECD Countries Paris: OECD, (2003) pp.99-126.

23. op. cit. 18

24. Graham, Carol Lee "From Safety Nets to Social Sector Reform: Lessons from the Developing Countries for the Transition Economies" in Joan M. Nelson, Charles Tilly & Lee walker, eds. Transforming Post-Communist Economies Washington DC: National Academy Press (1998).

25. Orenstein, Mitchell A. "How Politics and Institutions Affect Pension Reform in Three Postcommunist Countries" World Bank Policy Research Working Paper 2310, Washington DC: The World Bank (2000).

26. op. cit. 11

27. Müller, Katharina "Pension Reform Paths in Comparison" in Czech Sociological Review Vol.7, No.1, (1999) p.59)

28. Holzmann, Robert & Hinz, Richard "An International Perspective on Pension Systems and Reforms" Washington DC: The World Bank(2001).

29. Kitzer, Barbara E. "Social Security Reform in Central and Eastern Europe: Variations on a Latin American Theme" in Social Security Bulletin Vol.64, No.4, (2002) pp.16-32.

FAMILY AND CHILD SUPPORT IN A POSTCOMMUNIST SOCIETY: ORIGINS OF THE MIXED HUNGARIAN WELFARE CAPITALISM

DOROTTYA SZIKRA[1]

INTRODUCTION

Post-Soviet and Central and Eastern European countries have seen dramatic changes in the last 15 years in political, economic and social terms. Command-driven economic and labor market systems have been replaced by capitalist systems; one-party politics of state socialism have been replaced by democratic political systems. Yet, at the same time, changes in welfare systems were not as dramatic as other political and economic reforms. In Central and Eastern Europe the typical pattern is that welfare arrangements did not replace the previous systems with something entirely different, but rather they adjusted old welfare policies to the new circumstances. Thus, there is change and continuity in welfare policies and this proved to be a very important tool in most cases to prevent the majority of citizens from absolute deprivation that economic changes might have caused. Continued welfare provision has been an important tool in the hands of the new political elite, which sought to curb social unrest and avoid violent protest.

Hungary was one of the pioneering countries in publicly organised family policies around the turn of the last century. The pattern of continuity and change can already be seen after the Second World War, when instead of creating an entirely new system of welfare policies, the system of social insurance and cash-transfers for families was expanded and adjusted to the circumstances of the new socialist regime. Social policy (and social insurance within it) was probably one of the very few areas of relative continuity after 1948. The same pattern applies for the more recent changes: having changed but not diminished welfare systems after 1990, Hungary remained a long-time leader in family policy, which could serve as an example for other countries, especially post-Soviet states in the process of redesigning welfare institutions.[2]

The aim of this paper is to show the different aims and means of Hungarian family policies over the last century. This historical analysis of family policies will help us to better understand the genesis of the current system, which can be characterised as a mixed welfare regime with an expanded neo-liberal component. This complex system of cash-transfers coupled with the universal services for children over three provides assistance for all families and individuals with children. At the same time, the system is strongly biased towards the better off to the exclusion of the poorest groups, including the Roma.

Historical legacies, the effects of other countries and international organisations—such the World Band and the European Union—as well as new inventions have all had a hand in forming the current Hungarian family support system. The complexity of the current system raises questions as to whether it can be labelled with any of the classical attributes of Western welfare states. Using the terms of Esping-Andersen (1990), the system of welfare policies in Hungary is liberal and socialist and conservative—all at the same time. Also, placing Hungary in the feminist framework of "male breadwinner" and "dual breadwinner" models developed by Sainsbury (1996) is problematic. Some measures show a willingness of the state to increase women's participation in paid work and to share responsibilities of child-care with other family members, but others do not. Women with small children face discrimination in the labor market and tend to bear an unequal share of the domestic labor in families, which reflects a patriarchal pattern of welfare state.[3] Therefore, as analysts, it seems that we will need to reassess "old typologies" in an effort to create a new theoretical framework with which to analyze the historical development and the present welfare regimes in Central-Eastern European and post-Soviet countries.

FAMILY POLICIES UNTIL 1945

The welfare system in Hungary before the Second World War can be described as charity, and was essentially carried out by an extensive number of religious and non-religious private organisations; poverty alleviation policies carried out by the central and local state; and a Bismarckian-type of social insurance. The latter was, on the one hand, a response to industrialisation and, on the other hand, an attempt by the state to secure its legitimacy in an absolutist monarchy with rather limited suffrage. According to the argument of Flora and Alber, absolutist monarchies such as the Austro-Hungarian Empire were more likely to introduce social insurance legislation at an early stage of development.[4] Hungary is a model for this: it was among the first countries in Europe to introduce compulsory social insurance for industrial workers (in 1891 for illness and in 1907 for injuries) and the first country in Europe to introduce family allowance for civil servants in 1912.[5]

In the case of family allowance, there was a differentiation within the group of civil servants: the major share of family allowance went to those working in the Ministries and state administration. They received the allowance for a longer period, following the assumption that their children would study longer than the children of lower class public employees. This is a clear example of the state's role in preserving the position of social classes and groups, a characteristic of conservative welfare regimes.[6] I would call this period —until the 1930s—elitist family policy.

In 1919, the Hungarian Republic of Soviets aimed at a welfare and family policy based on social equality and institutional care. One of the main goals was to end the system of foster-parents, since children were extensively abused in these situations. Because of the very short period of the Republic (133 days) the original ideas never became reality, apart from some major holiday-programs for children.[7]

After the First World War, there was a general boom in social insurance measures throughout Europe, and Central and Eastern Europe was no exemption. Before the major 1928 Pension Act, pregnancy, child-bed and breast-feeding allowances were introduced in 1927 (Act XXI. 1927.). The duration of pregnancy and child-bed allowance was six weeks before and after the birth of the child and amounted to 100 percent of the previous income of the mother.

The Trianon Treaty after the First World War took two-thirds of the territories of Hungary away and one effect of this was increased nationalism, both in political and everyday discourse. Public social policy and social work of that time aimed at promoting the consciousness of the Hungarian nation in an openly nationalistic fashion. There were two parallel aims in this nationalist family policy: the first was to stop the decline of fertility rates. The second priority was to address the situation of peasant families, and was related to the first. According to the legislation on heritage, after the death of the father, land had to be divided between the children. As a consequence, hundreds of peasant families decided to have only one child in order to consolidate family property, especially in the southern region of Hungary.[8] Land consolidation was necessary because the land plots were already quite small, since 95 percent of landed property was in the hands of a few aristocratic and noble families. Thus, land reform was a priority, but finding a solution to the constant need for land without hurting the interests of the elite became a major part of the political agenda in the 1930s.

This period also saw a new societal policy, which had become strong and coherent by the second half of the1930s. It aimed at shifting the national distribution of wealth from the "rich Jews" to the "poor Christian working class." This national policy, accepted by almost the entire political elite, was called "changing of the guard." It soon led to discriminatory measures such as the first and the second "Act on the Jews," which created quotas for the Jewish minority in certain occupations and in higher education.[9] Jewish properties, both lands and factories, were partly nationalised and certain industries, mainly run by Jewish owners, were taxed to at extraordinarily high levels. This extra revenue allowed the government to introduce social policies (and within this, family policies) for the poor. Public health measures and land reforms (repartition of land) were introduced in 1936 with a clearly nationalist agenda.[10]

Another element of this societal and family policy was a new type of local social assistance, called "productive social policy." This set of measures enabled Hungarian Christian families to get loans for buying land, domestic animals or seeds in order to sustain themselves.[11] Although it was, for its time, a rather progressive way of helping the poor, its discriminatory basis and social control function is striking.[12] Also, the policy could only reach a minority of the agricultural population. In the rhetoric of the time, the notion of the "Hungarian nation" excluded Jews and the Roma and other ethnic minorities from social protection.[13]

Strengthening working class families was the aim of the introduction of family allowance for factory workers in 1938 (Act XXXVI).[14] The payment was very low, especially compared to that of the civil servants. It was paid until a child was 14 years old, which was the age that the state presumed that working-class children would begin to work.[15] In order to alleviate the economic crisis of the 1930s, workers received family allowance even after their loss of employment for a further three months.[16]

If we take the extensive growth of state-run social programs and the increasing importance of nation-wide charities into account, it is clear why some authors see the 1930s as a peak of welfare policies in Hungary.[17] At the same time, not much attention so far has been devoted to understanding how ethnic discrimination was linked to this extensive social policy before the Second World War in Hungary.[18]

FAMILY POLICIES UNDER STATE–SOCIALISM

1945–1965

Two distinct periods of social policy followed the end of the Second World War. The first is from 1945 to 1949, when democratic elections in 1947 showed broad support for improving social work and social policy measures that had been cut during the war. As Ferge describes, several efforts were made to create a complex societal policy, including a major repartition of huge pieces of land and building up a network of local social policy centers.[19]

Family allowance was extended to every industrial worker, and became part of the general social insurance scheme in 1946. The eligibility criteria and the amounts received were also unified: the distinction between public employees and industrial workers was eliminated. At the same time, agricultural workers were still excluded from social insurance legislation.

In 1949, after the Hungarian Workers' Party (MDP) gained power, a new agenda was set: no social policy was needed, it was argued, because the socialist political and economic mechanism would solve social problems automatically. Thus, in the 1950s, both social work as a profession and social policy as a discipline were abolished. At the same time, certain continuities can be traced in social policies. Social insurance and family provisions were not abolished but changed: their scope was gradually extended and their administration was centralised.[20] Social insurance was made a part of the central budget, under the control of the Party and the trade union (also being directed by the Party).

It must be noted that in the 1950s, general poverty was coupled with the violent control of individual lives and relationships.[21] Dramatically strict abortion legislation was introduced between 1950 and 1953, in order to meet the quantitative indicators set by Mátyás Rákosi, the head of MDP.[22] Women were to take up the double burden of productive paid work in the state sector and reproductive work within the family.[23] One of the means to achieve this was through social insurance and family policies linked to full time state-employment, preferably in the industrial sector.[24] Yet, women caring for many children or those who had dependant relatives and therefore could not take up full employment were not eligible for family provisions. Moreover, while family allowance and other provisions were provided for agricultural workers to a limited extent, it was not until 1975 that family allowance was made equal for agricultural workers. Evidence has emerged, which reveals that this policy was a deliberate but covert form of discrimination against the Roma.[25]

A 1953 order increased the number of crèches and kindergartens in the country. Still, there was not much improvement in the lives of Hungarian families during the 1950s, since living standards and life expectancy rates were very low. Fertility rates, having had after a short growth due to the strict anti-abortion legislation, nevertheless became the lowest in the world by 1962. I characterize the family policies described above as repressive and discriminatory, even though the extension of certain cash-transfers meant a clear development compared to pre-WWII.

The effects of the 1956 Revolution on welfare measures have not been examined yet. Still, it is clear that the 1960s saw a different pattern in social policies. After the revolution, a "covert agreement" was made between the political elite and the public. So-called "refrigerator socialism" was introduced, which meant that the top priority of the Party was to provide people with enough income to support a decent lifestyle. This was seen as the price of preventing political unrest. One of the major means to achieve this was an extensive set of welfare measures directed at families.

1965–1989

As concern over Hungary's extremely low fertility rates grew, the pressure on women to work was lessened during this period. Generous financial and service support was offered by the state to help women to reconcile the various responsibilities of work and childcare. At the same time, help was offered at different levels depending on class and race. Political discourse on Roma women and their fertility was very different from that of the non-Roma population.[26]

In 1967, a generous child allowance (GYES) was introduced for mothers who wanted to stay at home with their children in their first years and who had worked full time previously. For the first time, this policy gave a real possibility for women to choose between employment and domestic work. Agricultural workers (except those working in co-operatives) and non-state employees were excluded from this benefit. The time spent on child-allowance was considered as employment and was included in state contributions to the old-age pension scheme.

No other country in the world had introduced such a generous and long-term child benefit at that time. The reasons for introducing it in Hungary were many. Some argue that this was a way to create "hidden unemployment" during an economic slow-down. The desire to increase the fertility rate also played an important role in its introduction. Moreover, it was more cost-effective than maintaining crèches, which were expensive for the state. In addition, employers complained that mothers of young children either stopped working or had high absenteeism, which negatively impacted upon productivity.[27]

An income-related, higher-level childcare benefit (GYED) was the next step taken by the state as an incentive for better-off mothers to have more children. The replacement rate was 65 to 75 percent of salaries, depending on the years spent employed. There was (and still is) a possibility for women to choose between GYES and GYED. Since 1982, fathers became eligible for GYES as well, and mothers could take on part-time employment in addition to receiving the GYES. As Eva Fodor and her colleagues point it out, this measure was unique in the Central and Eastern European region, in that it enabled women to slowly adjust themselves to the labour market if they wished to return to it after childbirth.[28]

Having examined the state-socialist period more closely, it seems clear that social welfare was not at all homogenous. More simply, direct and sometimes forceful measures were focussed on families and women until the mid-1960s. From this time on, a more sophisticated and generous, work related family policy was initiated, which clearly made life easier for women. General economic stability and increased wealth due to extensive state-subsidies of goods were just as important as welfare measures in reaching this aim.

FAMILY SUPPORT SYSTEM IN THE NEW DEMOCRACY

After the economic and political changes in 1990, the family and child support system was kept in place and, in some cases, even expanded. At the same time, the universal benefits of the communist era lost value over the last 15 years, causing extensive poverty among low-income and unemployed families. The system became more complex as new forms of assistance were introduced. Many of the state-run crèches have been closed, but this did not cause a real fall in the percentage of children being placed in these institutions.[29] Universally available kindergarten for children between three and six years of age have been maintained as the possibility for mothers to free themselves partly from care-work and re-enter the labor market.

The system of cash-benefits created certain 'tracks' for families with different income levels. Family cash transfers have four major elements today, and are linked to different eligibility criteria so that they are targeted to distinct types of families:

1. Family allowance, for children up to the age of 18 and 25.
2. Two types of the previously described child allowances (GYED and GYES) and maternity benefits, connected to previous employment, which give incentives to parents to stay at home with their children until the age of 2 and 3.
3. Means-tested social assistance directed to poor families with children.
4. Tax credits.

Family allowance, which dates back to the turn of the last century, became universally available to all families (regardless of employment or income) in 1990. Its major intention has been to level the incomes of families with children, and to prevent poverty. This type of welfare assistance represents the wish to bear public responsibility for all children as they are held to be 'public goods'—investments into the future of the whole Hungarian society. The amount of the family allowance represented 3.1 percent of the GDP by that time, which was the highest in the world. With such a high level of family allowance, given as a universal right, this policy could be characterized as a 'socialist' type of welfare regime (Esping-Andersen, 1990). Yet, backed by widespread public consensus, the policy was introduced by a *conservative* government. It contributed to a great extent to the reduction of poverty, and especially child poverty in the very harsh period of transition.

At the same time, influential economists, such as János Kornai and international organisations, such as the World Bank criticized the policy as 'premature,' because of the relatively high level of social spending for universal family allowance and health care. It must be stressed here that the GDP was falling so sharply that the increase in the percentage of family allowance-spending (and, in general, welfare spending) meant that welfare spending decreased slightly less than the level of GDP.

Partly in response to this international pressure, in 1994, the Socialist-Liberal government introduced income-testing of family allowances and cancelled the GYED along with other cuts to welfare spending. The public's resistance to these measures was backed by the Constitutional Court, which deemed the austerity measures to be unconstitutional, citing that families have the right to a stable and calculable support system, which cannot be changed from one day to another. Thus, the introduction of cuts in family policies was delayed until 1996. It is also important to note that subsequent government did not raise the amount of the allowance along with inflation. Thus, by 1998, the share of welfare spending within the GDP fell to 1.2 percent.

The next Conservative government (with Fidesz—the Young Democrats as the leading party in the coalition) soon made family allowances universal again and re-introduced GYED, the social-insurance-based benefit for mothers with young children. Its amount, which is maximised at the level of the minimum wage, has been indexed with inflation since then. At the same time, this government let the amount of family allowance and GYES devaluate to an extent that has never been seen before. The share of family allowance from the GDP (which has been growing since 1997) was not more than 0.9 percent by 2002.

The "conservative" Fidesz government introduced new types of benefits in 1998, further strengthening the pattern of different tracks for low income and better-off families. A means-tested social assistance program for poor families and a tax-credit system for the better off were introduced. The share of the latter from the GDP reached 0.5 percent in 2002, more than double the amount devoted to means-tested social assistance. Poor families (those that do not have any taxable income) have been excluded from this type of assistance. It creates an unjust pattern of redistribution, since poverty rises with a greater number of children. Of the 77 percent of families with children who qualified to receive the full amount of the tax credit in 2003, most had one or two children.[30]

In the case of social assistance for the poor, home-visits to test the eligibility of families have been used extensively and the stigmatising practice has become even stronger over the years.[31] This might be one of the reasons why welfare assistance did not reach 57 percent of families belonging to the bottom third of the income scale.[32] It must be seen that the second conservative government was the first after 1990 to create a conscious family policy: their priority was to help people who 'work' and raise children at the same time and to foster employment through the taxation system.

When the Socialist-Liberal coalition gained power again in 2002, family allowance was not more than a universal poor relief as it only made a real difference in the budget of poor families. The government raised the amount of family allowance and GYES substantially in 2004 and announced plans to double the amount of family allowance from 2006. As a part of 'social democratic' family policy measures they want to abolish both social assistance for poor families and the family tax credit system. The aim is to make the system simpler and universally available. The fact that the tax-credit system would remain untouched for those who have three or more children, shows that the idea of a universal system is far from precise.

CONCLUSIONS

This paper demonstrated that there has been continuity and change in the Hungarian welfare system, and within that, family policy over the past century. Over the last 15 years, this process of continuity and change has led the Hungarian government to adopt a mixed-type of welfare regime, which simultaneously has the attributes of the socialist, liberal, and conservative welfare states, but also follows neo-liberal principals.

The elements of the family policy system are summarized here, with the help of the categories of Esping-Andersen (1990):

- 'Socialist' types of provisions are present through the universal family and child allowances, although their real value has decreased over time. A major step in the social democratic direction would be the possible doubling of the amount of family allowances proposed by the current government. At the same time, given the currently low level of these provisions, we can argue that the value of 'decommodification' is rather low. This means that welfare reformers may actually belong to the 'liberal' tradition.
- 'Conservative' elements have been present for a long time with the extensive, Bismarckian social insurance system, and within this, maternity and income-based child benefits, with a rather high replacement rate in the case of the GYED. At the same time, there has been a shift away from these types of provisions recently. Conservative or neo-liberal tendencies can be seen in the increased weight of tax-credit system.
- 'Liberal' elements have increasingly been present in the family and child support system over the last 15 years. First, when family allowance and GYES was made income-tested in 1996, for a short period, and later when means-tested assistance became increasingly important in line with letting the real value of universal provisions decline. Interestingly, the influence of the World Bank and the International Monetary Fund was less strong in the case of family policies than, for instance, the pension system. Less explicit policies (such as letting the real-value of family allowance fall) seem to indicate that the system is heading in a neo-liberal direction.

'Socialist'	'Liberal'	'Conservative'
Family allowance	Social assistance for children	Tax-credit system (?)
GYES		GYED

Universal family allowance and GYES, especially with the possibility to work while getting these benefits, provide the possibility for women to return to the labor market more easily. Means-tested child protection assistance is stigmatising, and this effects women more than men: it is overwhelmingly women who control families via home visits and women are the ones who are at home when these visits are made.[33] Abolishing this assistance and replacing it with double the amount of the universal family allowance would positively effect families, especially women and children.

The long time that can be spent on GYES and GYED (three and two years respectively) is good, on the one hand, because it provides stable income for women at home with their children. On the other hand, the employment of these women is only secured theoretically: women are easily and very often fired after returning from GYES and GYED, and they find it hard to get full-time employment. This is especially true for the lower classes: women with low level of education and Roma women can find it extremely difficult to get full-time, stable employment.

The Hungarian state has offered continuous support for all strata of families, particularly since the 1960s. The form of this support has been a unique combination of universalistic and paternalistic elements under state-socialism, with an increasing (but not exclusive) means testing after 1990. The relative continuity of the system made it possible to lessen the negative effects of the various political and economic crises of the 20th century, and especially the post-1990 transition period. If there is a positive message from the history of welfare arrangements in Hungary, it is this continuity. Maintaining family allowances and other cash benefits, alongside with extensive services for families has been very important, both for societal and political reasons. This welfare has eased the burden put on families by the new capitalist economy and has played a part in preventing political unrest.

At the same time, there are some negative aspects of the policy reforms that must be addressed. First, the Hungarian welfare state has shown clear discrimination against ethnic minorities, throughout the history of its welfare policies. In the early years of the Hungarian welfare state, these forms of discrimination were quite blatant, while later they were more covert. Today, for instance, the majority of Roma families are excluded from the tax-credit systems. Also, Roma children are discriminated against in kindergarten, and to an even greater extent in schools. Second, in an increasingly polarised political system, where there have been constant shifts in political power from left to right, both the conservative and the socialist parties (with their coalition partner, the liberals) have been trying to undo the reforms of their predecessors. This might not pay-off politically, since research suggests that people think that welfare is one of the country's most important values. Those with an average and low income find social security even more important than freedom.[34]

Constant reforms are especially dangerous in the family policy system, where volatility and unpredictability can diminish the positive effects of welfare policies. As experts suggest, the inconsistency of the system and its unpredictable and volatile manner made families more vulnerable and hurt their autonomy.[35] These programs also failed to reduce child poverty. Other experts, especially demographers, note that the same reasons added to the fact that fertility rates continue to fall.

ENDNOTES:

1. Dorottya Szikra, PhD is an associate professor of social policy at ELTE University, Budapest, Hungary, Department of Social Work and Social Policy, and a visiting professor at the Central European University, Budapest, Department of Gender Studies. E-mail: szikrasp@ludens.elte.hu The author is grateful for Adrian Sinfield for his useful comments and help.

2. It is important to see that these countries have at least as many differences as similarities. Recent literature clearly points this out: Eva Fodor – Christy Glass – Janette Kawachi – Livia Popescu (2002), "Family policies and gender in Hungary, Poland and Romania." In Communist and Post-Communist Studies 35. 475-490; Jolanta Aidukaite (2004), *The Emergence of the Post-Socialist Welfare State – the Case of the Baltic States: Estonia, Latvia and Lithuania*. Sodertorns hogskola, Stockholm.

3. Pateman, Carole (1988), "The Patriarchal Welfare State." Pp. 231-278. In Gutman, A. (ed.): *Democracy and the State*. Princeton University Press.

4. Flora, Peter – Jens Alber (1981), Modernization, Democratization, and the Development of Welfare States in Western Europe. In: Peter Flora/Arnold J. Heidenheimer (Eds.), *The Development of Welfare States in Europe and America*. New Brunswick: Transaction Books, pp37-80

5. The allowance was paid for men - women could only get family allowance in case the father died or was unable to work, or if the mother reared the child without any financial help from the father. Haller, Károly, Dr (1915), *A családi pótlékról szóló 1912. évi XXXV. Törvényczikk, és a reá vonatkozó rendeletek és határozatok gyűjteménye.* (Act XXXV. 1912. on family allowance and connected regulations.), Budapest. The allowance was paid for men - women could only get family allowance in case the father died or was unable to work, or if the mother reared the child without any financial help from the father.

6. Esping-Andersen, Gosta (1990), *The Three Worlds of Welfare Capitalism*. Polity Press, Cambridge.

7. Petrák, Katalin – Milei György (1959), *A Magyar Tanácsköztársaság szociálpolitikája*. (The social policy of the Hungarian Republic of Soviets.) Gondolat, Budapest.

8. This even has a special naming in Hungarian: "egyke", which means "one little".

9. Ungváry, Krisztián, "'Árjásítás' és 'modernizáció'". Adalékok Imrédy Béla miniszterelnöki müködéséhez és a zsidótörvények geneziséhez. *("Aryanization" and "modernization"*. Contributions to the activities of Béla Imrédy as prime minister and to the genesis of the acts on Jews.) In Századvég, Új folyam, 26. szám, 2002. 4. p18.

10. Tárkányi, Ákos, "Európai", p2.

11. It must be noted here that no other major social assistance program, be that public or charity was directed to families or mothers at this time.

12 On this issue see: Zimmerman, Susan, „Making a Living from Disgrace". The Politics of Prostitution, Female Poverty and Urban Gender Codes in Budapest and Vienna, 1860s – 1920s. In: Malcolm Gee, Tim Kirk, Jill Steward (eds), *The City in Central Europe: Culture and Society in Central Europe since 1800*. Brookfield, Ashgate, London 1999, pp. 175-195

13. Szikra, Dorottya – Varsa, Eszter (2005), "Gender, Class and Ethnicity-Based Differentiation in the Practice of Hungarian Social Work, A Case Study of the Kozma-Street Settlement, 1935-1945." In Kurt Schilde – Dagmar Schulte (eds.), Need and Care – Glimpses into the Beginnings of Eastern Europe's Professional Welfare. Barbara Budrich Publishers.

14. The first family allowance for workers was actually introduced in 1936, in the factory of French-Hungarian Cotton-Industry Ltd. owned by family Dewarvin. Tárkányi, p4.

15. Fluck, András (1939), *A munkások gyermeknevelési pótléka. A családi munkabér magyar intézménye*. (The child-raring allowance of workers. The Hungarian institution of family-wage. In. Mártonffy, Károly (ed.), *A mai magyar szociálpolitika*. (Hungarian social policy today.) Budapest, Keresztes-Fischer Ferenc. Quoted by Tárkányi, "Európai...", p4.

16. Another "solution" was to pay a longer sickness leave for workers. This, in turn, drove the national sickness insurance fund close to bankrupcy.

17. Tomka, Béla (2004), Welfare in East and West: Hungarian Social Security in an International Comparison, 1918-1990. Berlin: Akademie Verlag. *Szociálpolitika a 20. századi Magyarországon európai perspektívában.* (Hungarian social policy in the 20st century in a European perpective.) Századvég, Budapest.

18. The only example is Ungváry, "Árjásítás".

19. Ferge, Zsuzsa (1986), *Fejezetek a magyarországi szegénypolitika történetéből*. (Chapters of Hungarian Poor Policy.) Magvető, Budapest.

20. Ferge, Zsuzsa (1979), A Society in the Making. Hungarian Social and Societal Policy, 1945-1975. White Plains, N.Y.

21. By no means is Lynne Haney right when labelling this period "welfare society". This label hides the discriminatory and repressive manner of the system. Lynne Haney (2002), *Inventing the Needy. Gender and the Politics of Welfare in Hungary.* University of California. Press. Berkely, etc. 2002.

22. Kiss, Adrienn (2005), "Szemelvények az 1950-es évek abortuszpolitikájából." (On the abortion policies of the 1950s.) Manuscript. May, 2005.

23. Zimmerman, Susan (2003), "A szabad munkaerő nyomában. 'Utólérő' fejlődés és női munka Magyarországon. (In the search for free labour force. 'Catching-up development and female work in Hungary.) Eszmélet, 25, 1994-1995. Fodor, Éva, *Working Difference. Women's Working Lives in Hungary and Austria, 1945-1995.* Durham and London, Duke University Press.

24. Szalai, Júlia (1998), "A társadalombiztosítás érdekviszonyairól". (On the network of interests behind social insurance.) In. Szociológiai Szemle.

25. Varsa, Eszter (2005), Class, Ethnicity and Gender – Structures of differentiation in state socialist employment and welfare politics, 1960-1980. In. Shilde-Schulte: Need and Care…

26. "A cigánylakosság helyzetének megjavításával kapcsolatos egyes feladatokról. Az MSZMP KB Politikai Bizottságának határozata, 1961. június 20." (Tasks connected to the improvement of the situation of the Gypsy population. Decree by the Polit Bureau of the Hungarian Socialist Workers' Party's Central Commettee.) In. Mezey, Barna (ed.), *A magyarországi cigánykérdés dokumentumokban, 1422-1985.* (The Hungarian Gypsy-question in documents.) Budapest, Kossuth, 1986. Quoted by Varsa, Eszter: "The Construction…"

27. Interviews conducted with the designers of the system Tímár, János and Miltényi, Károly by Tárkányi. In. Tárkányi, "Európai", p14.

28. Eva Fodor – Christy Glass – Janette Kawachi – Livia Popescu (2002), "Family policies and gender in Hungary, Poland and Romania."

29. Eva Fodor et.al.

30. Darvas, Ágnes – Mózer, Péter (2004), "Kit támogassunk?" (Whom should we support?) In Esély, 2004/6.

31. This process is described in a very detailed manner by Szalai: Szalai, Julia (2004), "A jóléti fogda." (The welfare jail). In Esély, 2004/6.

32. Ferge, Zsuzsa – Tausz, Katalin – Darvas, Ágnes (2002), *Fighting poverty and social exclusion. The case of Hungary.* ILO.

33. Home visits check the ability of women to care for dependatns and to do the housework 'properly'.

34. Ferge, Zsuzsa (2005), *Ellenálló egyenlőtlenségek.* (Prevailing inequalilties.) Speech held in the Hungarian Academy of Sciences. Budapest, April, 2005. Manuscript.

35. Darvas, Ágnes – Mózer, Péter (2004), "Kit támogassunk?"

THE POLITICS OF DECENTRALIZATION AND OUTCOMES FOR SOCIAL SERVICES IN POLAND

JANELLE KERLIN[1]

Poland's second round of decentralization, the 1999 public administration reform, was an immense undertaking that included administrative, political and fiscal decentralization, as well as the territorial re-division of the state. As one of the earliest postcommunist states to attempt sweeping reforms to mid-level government, Poland's experience can provide a valuable example to other states in the region contemplating similar reforms. Many of the lessons learned stem from the overarching lesson of this reform story—that how policymakers go about the process of reform development (i.e., the politics of reform) can have as much influence on reform outcomes as the policy prescriptions they are trying to follow. In the Polish case, influences from old and new institutional structures and constant international and domestic pressures often pushed policymakers to compromise on basic standards, which led to unintended outcomes. This study shows how the politics of decentralization in Poland shaped the administrative reform package and ultimately affected social service outcomes at the county and province level. It concludes by outlining the main lessons learned.

Poland's 1999 public administration reform reduced the number of provinces from 49 to 16, restored 373 counties, and decentralized public programs and services to these two levels. Broad goals focused on increasing citizen involvement and improving public services. Initial outcomes show that the reform did not meet these goals and the policies that were adopted had unintended consequences. For example, democratization was only minimally increased as the central government retained both revenue generating and revenue assignment authority over most functions, which severely limited autonomy at the county and provincial levels. Moreover, a number of functions intended for decentralization remained centralized, which limited the capacity of the new subnational governments. Though decentralization improved some services by bringing them closer to the recipients, poor funding did little to improve services in other ways and in some cases made them worse. The unintended consequences of the reform was that certain policies worked at cross-purposes, resulting in such outcomes as increased disparity in services across urban and rural areas. In addition, a detailed examination of the reform in the area of social services reveals that policy outcomes were uneven across different policy sectors.

This paper shows that the influence of different ideologies, interest groups and international pressures on Polish policy actors, which competed for attention and pushed reform in different directions, produced irrational outcomes and unintended policy consequences. Conflicting ideologies and pressures on policy actors, stemming from a variety of historical, institutional, political and international sources, resulted in compromises made by the ruling parliamentary coalition. In this study, I test the result of these unintended consequences of the politics of reform on outcomes for social service delivery in the new provinces and counties. Among other data, I rely on data results from a nation-wide, representative survey of Polish public social service offices on three levels of government conducted in summer 2000.

This study reveals that the politics of reform development involved tensions between competing interests within and outside the ruling coalition government. This manipulation resulted in compromise that led to a less than satisfactory outcome. I draw and build upon Schickler's concept of "disjointed pluralism" to explain this political process and resulting outcomes.[2] Disjointed pluralism refers to the idea that many different formal and informal coalitions, promoting a range of collective interests, drive choices made in legislatures and that the dynamics of reform development "derive from the *interactions* and *tensions* among competing formal and informal coalitions promoting several different interests."[3] Here the interactions and tensions that characterize the relationship between multiple interests drive processes of change that are ultimately reflected in legislative outcomes.

The overriding objective of this study is to show how the politics of decentralization in Poland not only shaped the reform package, but also how it affected social service outcomes at the county and provincial levels. It examines what happened to policy goals as they moved through the political process and were written as policy. It then takes the analysis a step further by examining the consequences of the policy that emerged from this process. The two-phase analysis is key because the irony of Poland's decentralization reform was not only that inconsistent goals were written into policy and resulted in unmet goals but also that policies that managed to follow consistent goals resulted in unintended outcomes because they worked at cross-purposes with other reform policies. By connecting the politics of decentralization with decentralization outcomes, this research bridges the divide in the decentralization literature between politics and outcomes.[4]

METHODS

This study's focus on both the politics of decentralization reform and its service outcomes necessitated the use of two different types of original data collection. Focused interviews were used to understand the politics of reform and survey questionnaires were used to assess outcomes. Between 2000 and 2001, a total of 23 focused interviews were conducted with important reform actors. Twelve interviews were conducted with eleven members of the Polish Parliament representing the four main political parties. Eleven interviews were conducted with eight government officials and one university professor who were directly involved in drafting the reform. Most of the government officials interviewed held high positions in central ministries at the time that the reform was developed, including the Ministry of Internal Affairs and Administration, the Ministry of Finance and the Ministry of Labor and Social Policy. Also, two interviews were conducted with the head of the reform—the former secretary of state and government plenipotentiary for state systemic reform.

Original data collection on reform outcomes in the area of social services was gathered through a nation-wide representative survey conducted during summer 2000 of directors of 200 public social service institutions on three levels of government. These institutions were directly or indirectly involved in programs for the mentally and physically disabled, orphans, families in crisis, juvenile delinquents and the elderly.[5] A Polish research institute, Pracownia Badań Społecznych, provided trained interviewers and initial data analysis.[6] Research was conducted 18 months after the reforms were first implemented in January 1999 and expectations for outcomes were moderated against the early timing of the study.[7] Document collection was also undertaken to supplement the original research on politics and outcomes of the reform.

THE POLITICS OF REFORM

At the time of the second round of public administration reform, the 1998 democratic parliamentary elections had just removed the Democratic Left Alliance (the left-leaning former communist party that had controlled the government for four years) and placed in power a tenuous coalition government made up of the Solidarity Electoral Action (AWS) and the Freedom Union (UW). Although they were both two center-right parties, there were great differences both between AWS and UW and within each party regarding the means and ends of many aspects of state policy, including public administration reform. There was, however, broad consensus within the coalition that reforms should be moved forward quickly to make use of the "window of opportunity" created by the support that had brought them into power. Resistance, however, quickly surfaced from central bureaucracies that were on the defensive because they did not want to give up more control and authority after losing quite a bit in the 1990 municipal reforms. Old provincial capital cities, often politically powerful, also resisted the loss in status that would inevitably come with the abolishment of many of the old 49 provinces. In addition, numerous county advocates demanded the return of their counties along historic lines and trade unions resisted reforms in their spheres of activity. Reformers were also more responsive to the Western international community (to which Poland wanted to belong), which had much more interest in influencing Poland's public administration reforms than during the first round of decentralization in 1990.

Political theory currently used to understand postcommunist politics, with some exceptions, is roughly divided between those drawing on a rational choice perspective and those using a new institutionalist[8] approach with an emphasis on path dependency. There is also a third camp, consisting mainly of political economists, who resist the idea that political theory based on consolidated democracies can be used to explain political processes in transitioning countries.[9] Scholars drawing on new institutionalism focus on path dependency created by historical legacies, structures and ideologies in place before policy formation.[10] Others using rational or public choice approaches examine the rational choices of actors working within institutions to explain policy outcomes.[11] Some scholars have begun to analyze postcommunist policies from both new institutionalist and rational choice perspectives. For example, Cain and Surdej evaluate stalled pension reforms in Poland using transitional politics (along the lines of historical institutionalism) and public choice. They state, "Our analysis of pension policy not only illustrates the importance of history and ideas on policy developments in Poland but more precisely shows how the mechanisms of democratic functioning manipulate this history and ideas."[12]

Prior attempts at building a theoretical framework specifically for understanding the politics of decentralization in Eastern Europe have focused on the identification of various explanatory concepts or main variables of change including historical legacies (pre-communist, communist, and sometimes postcommunist), ideas or ideology, institutions and geographic considerations.[13] The emphasis of these accounts on institutions and historical and ideological influences places them within the sphere of new institutionalism. Their main weakness lies in limited analysis of the "back kitchen of politics," where the deals and compromises are made, which shape final policy outcomes.

In this study, the determinants and outcomes of the second round of decentralization in Poland were best explained by drawing on the combination of rational choice and historical institutionalism found in disjointed pluralism. This theoretical framework proved to work well in the environment of postcommunist politics, since it was able to account for much of the political process and policy outcomes. Two exceptions were that it failed to take into consideration possible variance in the institutional design of democracies (i.e., different designs produce different numbers and kinds of veto points) and that it did not account for the phenomenon of exclusionary politics characteristic of transitioning democracies.[14]

Schickler's theory of disjointed pluralism borrows from both rational choice and historical institutionalist theories showing that a combination of the two provides a more complete understanding of processes that influence policy formation. Schickler notes that rational choice contributes to the idea that the goal-driven behavior of legislative members shapes institutional outcomes whereas historical institutionalism shows that institutions are "historical composites."[15] He tempers the linearity of path dependency often found in historical institutionalism with the goal-driven behavior of individual members. He states, "whereas path dependence suggests that legislative institutions likely will, in the long run, move toward a single organizational model, members' multiple goals have precluded such an outcome."[16] The result of combining these two processes suggests the creation of institutions that are unstable and even contradictory, rather than stable institutions as much of the rational choice literature suggests.

The three claims of disjointed pluralism drawn on in this study focus on the consequences of interactions and tensions among competing formal and informal interests. The first claim posits that, with a few exceptions, the political process by which institutional change occurs is not characterized by just one collective interest but by multiple interests promoted by different coalitions. The interaction between these coalitions determines the outcomes of institutional change. Often the result of such conflicting multiple interests is that a specific goal of a single interest may be compromised by concessions to other interests. The Polish reform offers a number of examples of this type of compromise to which reform politicians succumbed in order to get reforms passed.

The second claim posits that reform initiators establish a basis for cooperation among opposing legislators by defining proposals in a way that appeals to their interests. Though used less frequently, Polish politicians who were able to use this approach to bring opponents on board saw less change to their reform proposals. The third claim is that institutions created by past decisions develop constituencies committed to the preservation of power afforded that institution.[17] Schickler posits that this constrains reformers, which leads them to add on new institutions rather than abolish old ones. As will be shown in the Polish case, many of the constituencies built up around old communist structures offered stiff resistance when threatened by the reform. Often the result was that new structures were built but had limited power transferred to them.

Not addressed by Schickler's analysis is the role a country's specific democratic framework can have in structuring the power and behavior of reform actors. The Polish political system is particularly susceptible to veto points that create opportunities for the involvement of other reform actors. Veto points or gates are "institutions with the power to influence or block policy initiatives."[18] Multiple veto points allow a wide array of interests into the process, necessitating negotiations and compromises of disjointed pluralism. Thus, the type of political system, in terms of its veto points, structures the number and kinds of compromise outlined in disjointed pluralism.

Poland has a presidential–parliamentary political system defined by a dual executive, bicameralism, and proportional representation. These characteristics resulted in veto points that gave the government relatively limited control over parliament during development of the 1999 reform. The high number of veto points opened the door to competing interests and thus the need for negotiation and compromise to push the reform through. However, compromises that facilitated the passage of reforms resulted in unintended consequences and undermined some original goals of the reform. Indeed, the number and type of veto points shape the pattern of power distribution in a political system, which can affect reformers' strategies for policymaking[19] and ultimately policy outcomes.

The differing interests underlying the conflict and compromise found in Poland's 1999 administrative reform were the result of disparate ideologies and pressures on policy actors stemming from a variety of historical, institutional, political and international sources. An examination of these ideologies and the pressures of interest groups and international influences reveals their sources and the basis for the conflict found in the reform development process.

Ideologies

Neotraditionalism in the Polish postcommunist context refers to a general attitude that changes attributed to the communist party that significantly altered the "Polish" state of affairs were things that needed to be undone, "fixed," and restored to their original "natural" state. In this case it was a return to the decentralized system and territorial division of the state in place before communism. Restoration of self-governing counties that had been abolished by the Communist Party in 1975 was especially viewed as an important step in returning Poland to its rightful democratic structure. This desire to return to a historical public administration design, though most heavily influencing the number of counties and county government, was influential in other aspects of the reform as well.[20] Neotraditionalism was an ideology espoused by policy actors who were initiators of the reform.[21]

Neoliberalism was another ideology found among policy actors in the right coalition. During the early years of transition, neoliberalism was a predominant ideology guiding the transition to democracy and a free market in Eastern Europe. The economic prescription called for stabilization that reduced government subsidies and limited budget deficit, price and trade liberalization, privatization and, institutionally, an overall withdrawal of the state from the economy. Neoliberals believed there was a window of opportunity immediately after the fall of communism, when support for democracy and new reforms was high, when citizens would tolerate the difficult, immediate side effects of reforms and later reap their benefits.[22] To take advantage of this window and shield reformers from possible opposition, reforms were hastily prepared by a closed team of experts. This was the course of action taken by Polish finance minister Leszek Balcerowicz and other neoliberals in their implementation of "shock therapy" in the early 1990s.

This approach to policymaking set a precedent for Balcerowicz and other neoliberals when they returned to the Ministry of Finance in fall 1998 and began work on the public administration reform. In behavior not captured by Schickler's theory of disjointed pluralism, they again instituted a closed-door policy during reform development that resulted in serious consequences for the entire public administration reform. Indeed, neoliberal inclinations were partly to blame for why fiscal decentralization did not take place as planned and was mainly responsible for a temporary fiscal plan that failed to adequately fund newly decentralized tasks and services. In addition, the right coalition's ideology of hasty reform preparation, intended as a strategy to outpace potential opponents, was later blamed in part for unclear and inconsistent legislation and poor initial outcomes. These results were an effect of neoliberal thinking that was not limited to fiscal aspects of reform development.[23]

Interest Groups

Interest groups sprang up almost immediately to block certain aspects of the reform or to promote policies that supported their interests. These groups included central bureaucrats, trade unions and defenders of old provincial capitals, county advocates and local government associations.

Reform and removal of the old communist bureaucratic apparatus was a priority for reformers for political reasons—to de-communize the administrative bureaucracy and put government responsibilities more directly under the control of the people (though also motivated by neotraditionalism). Many ministerial duties and special administrations were also to be transferred to elected county and provincial governments.

Given this pointed attack on the existing public administration system, it was no surprise that central bureaucracies put up considerable resistance during reform development. The devolution of control over ministerial tasks meant a significant loss of jobs and power for ministries. In addition, reformers needed to contend with the mentality that if an administrative task was important it should stay in the hands of the state administration and not be passed to "incompetent" locally elected officials. Outcomes in this area differed largely according to the political influence of a given ministry and the willingness of reformers to compromise in exchange for a minister's support of the reform as a whole.[24]

Several trade unions were also staunchly opposed to administrative decentralization in their respective areas. Decentralization for them meant loss of influence over issues currently controlled in the center and thus also loss of bargaining power with the central government. Two unions in particular, the Solidarity Labor Union and the Polish Teachers Union,[25] were able to significantly influence the reform process in the area of decentralization though with differing degrees of impact on outcomes.

A strong lobby was also created by inhabitants of old provincial capitals that stood to lose their status with the reform. Reformers initially established the optimal number of provinces at 12, which meant the abolishment of 37 provincial capitals. Residents of these capitals feared the loss of jobs and resources that would follow and protested by organizing rallies in front of parliament and in extreme cases by blocking roads and railway lines.[26] Such pressure was largely responsible for the establishment of 16 rather than 12 provinces and resulted in compensation to abolished provincial capitals giving them status as both municipalities and counties among other things.

There were also numerous county groups that sprang up to promote the return or creation of a county in their area. These groups traveled to Warsaw and petitioned parliamentary committees directly for their counties. Lawmakers, in their quest for political support, all too often acquiesced to their requests even though it pushed the number of counties far beyond the recommended number.

International Influence

International influence on the public administration reform came in various forms. First, there was the soft influence of western ideologies and ideas that were adopted by reformers. This included neoliberalism espoused by foreign advisors to Poland from the early transition period but also supported by more long-term players such as the World Bank and the International Monetary Fund (IMF). Ideas on decentralization, especially in terms of subsidiarity, were put forward by the European Union and indirectly encouraged in country assessments. A host of other international organizations were influential in their dissemination of ideas about and support for decentralization. The United States Agency for International Development (USAID) funded full-time American advisors and other consultants to work with reformers, most significantly the Ministry of Finance, on developing legislation for fiscal decentralization (though advice in this area went largely unused).[27]

Second, there existed a kind of international influence of the 'carrot' variety. That is, European Union aid in the form of structural assistance and the ability to compete economically on the same level with other large regions in Western Europe were great incentives for Poland to create a complementary regional system. Third, international influence on the reforms came in the more direct form of the Council of Europe's charters on local and regional government, signed by Poland, which directly call for elected self-governments on subnational levels.

These four influences each impacted the four different sub-debates of the reform (administrative, political, and fiscal decentralization and territorial division of the state) to varying degrees. Administrative decentralization was most influenced by a convergence of neotraditional ideology and international influences. Political decentralization was divided between the influence of neotraditional ideology on restored county self-government and international influences in the case of new provincial self-governments. Fiscal decentralization was dominated by neoliberal ideology and territorial division of the state was split between neotraditional ideology that drove up the number of counties and international influences that kept the number of provinces low. Looking at domestic and international factors overall, it appears that domestic politics may have had a slight edge when considering the reform as a whole, though international elements had a strong impact on key parts of the reform.[28] Interestingly, due to the inter-relatedness of the four parts of the reform, analysis found that the politics of each influenced outcomes for the other parts of the reform as well.

OVERVIEW OF SOCIAL SERVICE OUTCOMES

The preceding discussion uncovered ways in which large scale pressures and processes impacted on the public administration reform as a whole. However, each public service area was affected not only by these more macro-scale events but also by processes specific to the service area. Analysis of policy and outcomes in the area of social service delivery illustrate how both overarching reform policy and service specific policy affected outcomes for citizens.

The social services under consideration here mainly include those benefits and programs that were decentralized to or newly established on county and provincial levels.[29] On the county level this includes all types of social assistance homes and the new County Family Assistance Center responsible for crisis intervention, specialized counseling, services for the disabled, foster care, and community integration services for youth, among others. Provinces, rather than administer programs, were entrusted with regional development and education programs for social services with the addition of a provincial social service administrative office under the auspices of new provincial self-government. Old, centrally run provincial offices retained their monitoring and supervisory role.

The public administration reform in Poland was undertaken largely on the basis of expected improvements to democracy and public services and its broader goals are easily applied to the social service context:

Democracy
    A) Increased decentralization of social service tasks;
    B) Appropriate and rational funding for social service tasks;

C) Increased influence of civil society and societal control over social services;

D) Increased influence of democracy (county elections) on county social service tasks.

Improved Public Services

A) Improvement in social services in terms of distance and accessibility;

B) Improvement in the clarity of the competency system and flow of information;

C) Addition of regional politics and planning in the area of social services;

D) Improvement in the level of professionalism in local social services.

An analysis of the policies that created the new social service delivery system shows that they did not always achieve the stated goals of the reform. Policies fell into three categories: deviant policy (policy that did not achieve its intended goal); counterproductive policy (policy that addressed the intended goal but worked at cross purposes with other goals); and expected policy. The following is a summary of social service outcomes based on a nationwide survey of public social service offices and other sources.

Deviant Policy

The large-scale reform processes in the area of fiscal policy resulted in unmet reform goals with respect to social services. The fiscal policy was intended to cover the needs of decentralized services and provide for the autonomous (potentially democratic) functioning of subnational units—that is, that citizens, through their local governments, would be more involved in decisions regarding decentralized services. Due to the politics of the reform, administrative tasks were decentralized but fiscal responsibility was not, which effectively retained decision-making power regarding services on the central level. Most dramatic for social services was the situation in counties. Though counties had been given complete fiscal responsibility for a number of social services, on average less than 5 percent of a county's budget was made up of its own revenues.[30] The result was a drastic underfunding of social services where regular counties were only able to meet 21 percent of need for such services while urban counties could meet 47 percent of the need, according to the survey. The problem stemmed from the fact that subnational governments were not provided with sufficient revenue generating capacity nor adequate shares in centrally-controlled personal income tax (PIT) and corporate income tax (CIT) to finance tasks for which they had been given fiscal responsibility.[31] Thus, the temporary fiscal policy put in place with the reform was not in harmony with its goals of adequate funding of subnational services and improved democracy as limited fiscal autonomy translated into limited political autonomy.

Counterproductive Policy

Counterproductive policy is policy that, while achieving its immediate goal, worked at cross-purposes with other goals of the reform. For instance, decentralization policies, which brought government closer to the people, came into conflict with the goal of creating an efficient public administration. This conflict in policy was often the result of the overall administrative structure and circumstances found specific to certain service areas, including: social services. Counterproductive policies found here included: the creation of cities with county status that led to increased disparity between urban and rural services; policy regarding provinces that led to centralization of provincial offices and inefficient intergovernmental functioning; decentralization of some specialized services to small county units that resulted in an inefficient economy of scale for those services; policy that allowed for county presidents to hire county center directors, which opened the door for politicization and corruption; and decentralization of social assistance homes that resulted in an inefficient system of funding for those homes.

Expected Policy

Expected policy is understood as policy that shows progress in reaching goals and that does not conflict with other goals of the reform. Given the early nature of the study, indeed, any movement towards achievement was deemed an indication that expected policy had been implemented. The analysis of survey results found indicators that goals of the reform to stimulate civil society, establish increased societal control (oversight) over public services, and bring services closer to citizens were starting to be realized through specific social service policy and activities. This was based on survey evidence that new county family assistance centers were cooperating with municipal social assistance centers and non-governmental social service organizations, that half of all county centers were making use of a needs assessment and goal planning instrument and involving the community in its preparation, and that specific decentralized social services had indeed been brought closer to citizens.

A MODEL FOR DECENTRALIZATION POLITICS AND POLICY OUTCOMES

The particular political environment in which decentralization policy was generated in Poland resulted in several types of politics, which corresponded to the different kinds of policy outcomes outlined above. Exclusionary politics of neoliberals resulted in deviant policy. Contested politics, best explained by disjointed pluralism, resulted in counterproductive policy. Largely uncontested but uninformed politics also had the outcome of counterproductive policy. Uncontested politics resulted in more or less expected policy (see Table 1). This model is based on the perspective of reform initiators. Thus, while they would view policy outcomes as deviant or counterproductive, other actors (i.e., neoliberals, interest groups) may view the very same outcomes as positive.

Table 1: Types of politics and corresponding policy outcomes for decentralization in Poland

Type of Politics	Exclusionary	Contested	Uncontested—Uninformed	Uncontested
Policy Outcome	↓ Deviant	↓ Counterproductive	↓ Counterproductive	↓ Expected

The model of politics and corresponding policy outcomes was created on the basis of inductive observation of the study's empirical data informed by political theory. Its purpose is to show general trends in politics and outcomes for this particular decentralization reform in its specific political context. Though the model is therefore not intended as a theory, it can be viewed as a theoretical proposition to be investigated by future comparative studies of postcommunist countries. Factors that may limit the generalizability of the Polish case to other postcommunist states include its status as a first wave country for accession to the European Union, its relatively homogenous make-up (it lacks a sizable ethnic minority), and the fact that its public administration reform was more far reaching in breadth and depth than in other postcommunist countries. The following is a description of each of the model's categories for type of politics and corresponding policy outcome.

Exclusionary politics occurs when policymakers (in this case neoliberals) limit the participation of other groups in the policy-making process in order to achieve policy outcomes they have prescribed. According to Haggard and Kaufman, this narrow approach to policy making may interfere with the actual undertaking of a reform initiative.[32] Exclusionary politics in Poland was part of the reason why fiscal decentralization was stalled, which produced a policy that deviated from the original reform goal. In addition, self-isolating policymakers were in a position to manipulate this substitute reform to their own ends, resulting in another deviant policy. *Deviant policy* is policy that did not achieve original reform goals.

Contested politics occurs when coalitions promoting different interests force compromise that moves policy into an unintended direction. This type of politics is informed by Schickler's theory of disjointed pluralism, which shows how tensions and interactions of different interest coalitions in legislative politics can result in unstable and contradictory institutions. Here, such policy outcomes were labeled *counterproductive,* in the sense that though they may have addressed a goal of the reform they worked at cross-purposes with other goals.

Uncontested-uninformed politics are politics that, though minor conflict is present, the majority opinion moves reform in the direction originally intended by reformers with little or no compromise to the basic premise of the reform. However, this also often means that policymakers are uninformed about the possible negative consequences of reform on a specific policy or how to create the best policy for a particular policy area. This type of politics is informed by the literatures on the cognitive limitations of policymakers and the specific policymaking environment found in transitioning countries.[33] It also results in counterproductive policy as defined above. *Uncontested politics* are those in which conflict between competing interests is minimal, precluding the need for compromise and where policymakers are relatively informed *OR* are not informed entirely but their gamble with the policy they initiate pays off.[34] In the case of Polish reform, the result of such politics was *expected policy* understood as policy that shows progress in reaching goals and does not conflict with other goals of the reform.[35]

CONCLUSIONS

Major decentralization reforms in a postcommunist, democratic context, when studied from when the goal is adopted through policy design and implementation, were found in this study to be far more determined by the politics of reform than by prescriptions of Polish policy experts. While goals may reflect desired outcomes anticipated by experts, realization of them is subject to the realities of conflicting interests and limited resources, both intellectual and financial. Indeed, though the goals of decentralization in Poland called for the improvement of both democracy and efficiency, it is interesting to find that reformers, at times inadvertently, advanced the goal of subnational democracy (through the establishment of self-governing provinces and an unexpectedly large number of counties with self-governance) over the goal of efficiency when the two came in conflict. That this large subnational decision-making structure was then partially undermined by lack of fiscal decentralization points to an interesting phenomenon in democratic governance in Poland. On the one end are neoliberals, who seek to limit involvement in policymaking with the justification that they know what is best for all. On the other end are politicians, who allow the preferences of citizens to determine policy far beyond rational ideas of what is in the best interest for all. Thus, the question of how much democracy to allow into the policymaking process is an issue with which Polish lawmakers still appear to be grappling. Meanwhile, the results of these extreme approaches are being reflected in policy outcomes.

The Polish case provides a number of interesting lessons for policy-makers attempting state administrative reforms in other postcommunist countries. As stated previously, the overarching lesson of the Polish experience is that the process involved in making policy is just as important as the initially prescribed content of that legislation when considering reform outcomes. Following this theme, some of the specific lessons of the Polish reform are as follows:

THE POLITICAL PROCESS:

1) Newly elected parties in consolidating (as opposed to early transitioning) democracies, cannot rely as much on the "window of opportunity" they had immediately after winning (when support for their reforms appears to be high) to push forward reforms. Potentially conflicting interests appear to have more stakeholders and power when democracy is established and players have oriented themselves in the new democratic system. International influences are also stronger.

2) When working on a large, multifaceted reform, the politics of one part of the reform and the resulting poor policy can negatively impact upon outcomes for other parts of the reform.

3) Without careful reform preparation and oversight, policies in one part of the reform can work at cross-purposes with policies in other parts of the reform and undermine outcomes even when they are successfully achieving their own discreet outcomes.

4) Insisting on transparency in national-level policymaking may help prevent exclusionary policymakers from commandeering key elements of the reform.

5) Citizen education on outcomes of different reform options may help policymakers find the support they need to balance subnational democracy and efficiency considerations and achieve sought after outcomes.

EASILY OVERLOOKED POLICY CONSIDERATIONS:

1) Fiscal decentralization must occur for true decision-making power to be achieved on the subnational level.

2) The decentralization of both tasks and the funding responsibility for them should be matched by the decentralization of fiscal mechanisms to generate revenue for the support of such tasks.

3) Decentralizing social services appears to stimulate civil society activity in newly created subnational governments.

4) Decreasing the number of existing mid-level government units effectively centralizes the services offered on that level in relation to lower levels of government.

6) Combining two levels of subnational government units into one unit (in the Polish case these were the cities with county status) may create or exacerbate disparities between that unit and neighboring areas that are not combined.

ENDNOTES:

1. Paper based on research funded by a Fulbright-Hays Dissertation Research Abroad Fellowship and an American Council of Learned Societies East European Dissertation Fellowship.

2. For a discussion on the utility of disjointed pluralism versus collective interest see Eric Schickler, *Disjointed Pluralism: Institutional Innovation and the Development of the U.S. Congress* (Princeton: Princeton University Press, 2001).

3. Schickler, *Disjointed Pluralism*, 4.

4. This paper is based on the author's book, *Social Service Reform in the Postcommunist State: Decentralization in Poland* (College Station, TX: Texas A&M University Press, 2005). Please refer to the book for a fuller discussion of the topics in this paper.

5. Institutions in the study included 66 municipal social assistance centers, 70 county family assistance centers, 32 city family assistance centers, all 16 provincial departments of social affairs and all 16 provincial regional social policy centers. The survey provided information on degree of reform implementation, funding levels, civil society activity (including involvement of non-governmental organizations), professionalization of the social service sector, and intergovernmental cooperation and coordination. On county and provincial levels, self-administered questionnaires consisting of close-ended questions were delivered by an interviewer who remained present during survey completion. Surveys conducted in municipalities were done by computer-assisted telephone interviewing (CATI) using fixed-response questions.

6. Funding for the surveys and interviews conducted in 2000 was provided by a Fulbright-Hays Dissertation Research Abroad Fellowship 1999-2000. Interviews

conducted in 2001 were funded by an American Council of Learned Societies East European Dissertation Fellowship.

7. See chapter 5 in Kerlin, *Social Service Reform in the Postcommunist State,* for a more detailed description of the survey methodology used here.

8. New institutionalism is a branch of public policy analysis "concentrated on identifying key institutional features that affect the way in which actors interact in the formulation of policy, and as a result have an impact on policy outcomes," Giuliano Bonoli, *The Politics of Pension Reform: Institutions and Policy Change in Western Europe* (Cambridge: Cambridge University Press, 2000), 39. Historical institutionalism and path dependency are subsumed under new institutionalism.

9. Michael Cain and Aleksander Surdej, "Transitional Politics or Public Choice? Evaluating Stalled Pension Reforms in Poland," In L. Cook, M. Orenstein, and M. Rueschemeyer, eds., *Left Parties and Social Policy in Postcommunist Europe* (Boulder, CO: Westview Press, 1999).

10. Stephan Haggard and Robert Kaufman, *The Political Economy of Democratic Transitions* (Princeton: Princeton University Press, 1995); Samuel Huntington, *The Third Wave: Democratisation in the Late 20th Century* (Tulsa: University of Oklahoma Press, 1991); Juan J. Linz and Alfred Stepan, *Problems of Democratic Transition and Consolidation: South America and Post-Communist Europe* (Baltimore: Johns Hopkins University Press, 1996); S. White, J. Blatt, and P. Lewis, eds., *Developments in East European Politics* (New York: Macmillan and Co., 1993); Valerie Bunce, "The Political Economy of Postsocialism," *Slavic Review* 58, no. 4 (1999): 756-793.

11. Alberto Alesina, "Political Models of Macroeconomic Policy and Fiscal Reforms," In S. Haggard and S. Webb, eds., *Voting for Reform: Democracy, Political Liberalization, and Economic Adjustment* (Oxford: Oxford University Press, 1994); M. Kaminski, G. Lissowski, and P. Swistak, "The 'Revival of Communism' or the Effect of Institutions? The 1993 Polish Parliamentary Elections," *Public Choice* 97, no. 3 (1998): 429-450; Mancur Olson, "The Devolution of Power in Post-Communist Societies: Therapies for Corruption, Fragmentation and Economic Retardation," In R. Skidelsky, ed., *Russia's Stormy Path to Reform* (London: Social Market Foundation, 1995); Adam Przeworksi, *Democracy and the Market* (Cambridge, UK: Cambridge University Press, 1991).

12. Cain and Surdej, "Transitional Politics or Public Choice?," 146.

13. Martin Brusis, "Re-creating the Regional Level in Central and Eastern Europe: An Analysis of Administrative Reforms in Six Countries, In Erik von Breska and Martin Brusis, eds., *Central and Eastern Europe on the Way into the European Union* (Munich: Center for Applied Policy Research, 1999); Michal Illner, "Territorial Decentralization – A Stumbling Block of Democratic Reforms in East-Central Europe?" *Polish Sociological Review* 1, no. 117 (1997): 23-45; Joachim J. Hesse, "Rebuilding the State: Public Sector Reform in Central and Eastern Europe," In Jan-Erik Lane, ed., *Public Sector Reform: Rationale, Trends and Problems* (London: Sage, 1997); Hellmut Wollman, "Institution Building and Decentralization in Formerly Socialist Countries: The Cases of Poland, Hungary,

and East Germany," *Environment and Planning C: Government and Policy* 15, (1997): 463-480.

14. Bela Greskovits, *The Political Economy of Protest and Patience.*

15. Eric Schickler, *Disjointed Pluralism: Institutional Innovation and the Development of the U.S. Congress,* 267.

16. Ibid., 268.

17. See also Paul Pierson, *Increasing Returns, Path Dependence, and the Study of Politics* (Typescript, Howard University, 1998); Douglass North, *Institutions, Institutional Change, and Economic Performance* (Cambridge, UK: Cambridge University Press, 1990); Thomas F. Remington and Steven S. Smith, "Theories of Legislative Institutions and the Organization of the Russian Duma," *American Journal of Political Science* 42, (1998): 545-72.

18. Stephan Haggard and Robert Kaufman, "Introduction," In J. Kornai, S. Haggard, and R. Kaufman, eds., *Reforming the State: Fiscal and Welfare Reform in Post-Socialist Countries* (Cambridge, UK: Cambridge University Press), 16.

19. Bonoli, *The Politics of Pension Reform;* Haggard and Kaufman, "Introduction."

20. Jerzy Regulski, "Nowy Ustrój, Nowe Szanse, Nowe Problemy." In *Podstawowe Wartości i Założenia Reformy Ustrojowej – Ustrój Samorządu Terytorialnego w Polsce* (Warsaw: Chancellory of the President of the Council of Ministers, 1999); Włodzimierz Puzyna, interview with author, Warsaw, July 6, 2000; P. Fenrych and W. Puzyna, "Wielka Decentralizacja." *Więź* 6, no. 512 (2001): 14-28; Zyta Gilowska, "Reforma Samorządow a Reforma Finansów Publicznych," In Lena Kolarska-Bobinska, ed., *Cztery Reformy: Od Koncepcji do Realizacji* (Warsaw: Oficyna Naukowa, 2000).

21. Neotraditionalists included parliamentary representatives who had worked in local government and had the continuation of decentralization as their specific goal when they entered parliament in 1998. They were found mostly in the governing right coalition (AWS) but also among representatives of the *Democratic Left Alliance.*

22. Mitchell Orenstein, *Out of the Red: Building Capitalism and Democracy in Postcommunist Europe* (Ann Arbor: University of Michigan Press, 2001).

23. Michał Kulesza, the government plenipotentiary for the reform, acknowledges that the speed of the reform undermined its quality, however, in his view, speed was the only way to get ahead of the opposition and pass the reform at all. He states, "...the radical changes had to be implemented in a democratic way and that is why an emperor's power had to be replaced with high pace of work as only speed could save us. That was why, my aim was to implement the reform even when quality would suffer." See Michał Kulesza, "Methods and Techniques of Managing Decentralization Reforms in CEE Countries: The Polish Experience," In Gábor Péteri, ed., *Mastering Decentralization and Public Administration Reforms in Central and Eastern Europe* (Budapest: Local Government and Public Service Reform Initiative/Open Society Institute, 2002), 205.

24. Emilewicz and Wołek, *Reformatorzy i Politycy;* Włodzimierz Puzyna, interview with author, Warsaw, July 6, 2000.

25. In Polish, *Związek Nauczycielstwa Polskiego.*

26. Andrzej Kowalczyk, "Local Government in Poland," In T. Horvath, ed., *Decentralization: Experiments and Reforms* (Budapest: Local Government and Public Service Reform Initiative/Open Society Institute, 2000); Jolanta Koral, "Sukcesy i Porażki Wdrażanej Reformy," In Lena Kolarska-Bobinska, ed., *Cztery Reformy: Od Koncepcji do Realizacji* (Warsaw: Oficyna Naukowa, 2000).

27. Other technical assistance for the reform, including expert conferences and study trips to West European countries, was provided by International Policy Services (contracted by the Commission of European Communities), the International Investment Fund, the World Bank, DATAR (department of the French government), the French-Polish Foundation, the Swedish Agency of International Development, and the British Know How Fund. The EU's PHARE program eventually funded training for local governments and monitoring and analysis of the reform. Kulesza, *Sprawozdanie z Działalnośći Pełnomocnika Rządu ds. Reform Ustrojowych Państwa.* For a discussion on the role of western assistance on local democracy reforms in Poland through 1997 see Joanna Regulska, "Building Local Democracy: The Role of Western Assistance in Poland," *Voluntas: International Journal of Voluntary and Nonprofit Organizations* 9, no. 1 (1998): 39-57.

28. For a broader discussion on the varying impact of these influences on each of the reform subdebates see chapter 4 in Kerlin, *Social Service Reform in the Postcommunist State.*

29. Some reference is made to secondary effects of the reform to the municipal level in the area of social service delivery though the reform did not legally alter municipal legislation.

30. Związek Powiatów Polskich, *Monitorowanie Działalności Powiatów Polskich – Raport 1* (Nowy Sącz: Związek Powiatów Polskich, 1999).

31. Tony Levitas and Jan Herczyński, "Decentralization, Local Governments and Education Reform in Post-Communist Poland," (Paper prepared for the Open Society Institute's Local Government Initiative Program, 2001). Fiscal decentralization in Poland and Europe generally includes both the transfer of revenue generating authority to lower levels and any funds subnational governments are given which they are free to spend as they choose. This includes subnational government shares in PIT and CIT (collected and disbursed on the central level) not earmarked for specific purposes by the central government (see Levitas and Herczyński, "Decentralization, Local Governments," footnote 29).

32. Haggard and Kaufman, "Introduction." See also Béla Greskovits*, The Political Economy of Protest and Patience,* (Budapest: Central European University Press, 1998) for a discussion on economic reformers in transitioning countries who fail to consult and negotiate with outside actors and use secrecy to achieve their ends.

33. Schickler, *Disjointed Pluralism,* 268. See also David Braybrooke and C. Lindblom, *The Strategy of Decision: Policy Evaluation as a Social Process* (New York:

Free Press of Glencoe, 1963); J. March and H. Simon, *Organizations* (New York: Wiley, 1958) ; Charles Lindblom, "The Science of Muddling Through," *Public Administration Review* 14, (1959): 79-88; John Kingdon, *Agendas, Alternatives, and Public Policies* (New York: HarperCollins College Publishers, 1995); Mitchell Orenstein and Martine Haas, "The Global Politics of Attention and Social Policy Transformation in East-Central Europe." (Paper presented at the Annual Meeting of the American Association for the Advancement of Slavic Studies, 2000).

34. Lindblom in particular addresses this "flying by the seat of one's pants" method of policymaking in Lindblom, "The Science of Muddling Through," 79-88.

35. For specific examples of reform events that illustrate these types of politics and their corresponding policy outcomes as well as a much broader treatment of the subject of this paper see the author's book, *Social Service Reform in the Postcommunist State: Decentralization in Poland* (College Station, TX: Texas A&M University Press, 2005).

THE POLITICS OF INSTITUTIONALIZED VOLATILITY: LESSONS FROM EAST CENTRAL EUROPEAN WELFARE REFORMS

BÉLA TOMKA

While there can be little doubt about the direction of economic transformation of postcommunist East Central Europe, there have been considerable differences of opinion among social scientists about the character of the new welfare regimes and the trends of welfare development in the region. In the early to mid-1990s, most experts conceptualized the transformation of welfare systems in the framework developed by G. Esping-Andersen.[1] Many specialists expected the arrival of "conservative" and "social democratic" welfare regimes.[2] However, the majority of observers, including Esping-Andersen, have described the welfare reforms in postcommunist East Central Europe as being "liberal-capitalist."[3] Moreover, this discourse on the liberal transformation has been suffused with analysts' wishes and fears. Some observers have stressed the inevitability of welfare service privatization and have considered the communist legacy to be the leading obstacle to the liberal transformation they wished to achieve. At the same time, advocates of extensive social services emphasized the high social costs of the liberal reforms they feared.[4] Thus, while they may have had diverging ideals and conflicting arguments, these commentators have created a dominant narrative on East Central European welfare reforms, which describes the process as being sometimes overly hesitant, sometimes unnecessarily painful, but with a clear trajectory towards a "liberal" or "residual" welfare regime, in which variations mostly result from the level of a country's progress in that process.[5]

For the last couple of years, however, alternative interpretations have appeared in the literature. Welfare systems in postcommunist East Europe have been described as mixtures of different elements of Western European social democratic, conservative and liberal welfare regimes.[6] The dominance and irreversibility of liberal welfare policies has been questioned as well. These alternative interpretations argue that welfare policies in the new democracies have not followed a linear path, but have been volatile and often chaotic, due to the lack of consensus among experts or the public about the desirable direction of welfare reforms.[7] Here, I intend to present further evidence for the validity of this argument by considering the antecedents and causes of the "mixed" features and the volatility of East Central European welfare systems, focusing on the case of Hungary. I argue that the specific determinants of East Central European welfare systems in the second half of the 20th century greatly contributed to the present "mixed" characteristics of the region's welfare sectors and to the instability of the postcommunist welfare arrangements there, rather than simply resulting from the transition from a communist to a liberal welfare system.

The analysis presented here undeniably has some limitations. The focus is on the experience of Hungary, although I touch upon other East Central European countries (Czechoslovakia, its successor states and Poland) to a lesser degree. Despite the constraints, I find that the areas examined explain what the predispositions for welfare development in East Central Europe were, and this might also have relevance to the welfare research of the wider post-Soviet region. Thus, the approach might at least serve as a starting point for further more comprehensive studies.

THE POLITICS OF INCONSISTENCY: DETERMINANTS AND PRACTICE OF WELFARE IN COMMUNIST EAST CENTRAL EUROPE

Comparative welfare state research has produced a series of competing—but not necessarily mutually exclusive—interpretations of the emergence and development of welfare states in Western Europe.[8] It is not possible to fully summarize the vast literature on the subject here, but I will briefly refer to the most important pieces of welfare research.[9] Mainstream research has emphasized that, in Western Europe the impact of industrialization, the changing structure of the population and labor force, and—most importantly—the political mobilization of actors favoring extensive welfare programs were the major factors behind the rise of social rights. Political mobilization relied on forming class alliances in order to be effective. In turn, political mobilization also had social and cultural preconditions, such as associability or social capabilities to boost cooperation and effective collective action (such as trust etc.).[10]

I argue that some of these factors impacted welfare development both in East Central and Western Europe. Throughout Europe, there is undoubtedly a broad link between socio-economic and welfare development. This relationship is demonstrated by the employment structure, the transformation of which had long-term consequences on the growth of welfare programs. The dynamics of social policy development, however, seem to contradict any closer relationship between socio-economic and welfare development in East Central Europe.

The first social programs appeared in Hungary in 1892, which was quite a bit earlier than countries with high industrialization and urbanization levels, such as Belgium and Great Britain. Since industrialization in Hungary was lagging behind West European countries during this period, the early timing of the welfare programs is an anomaly from the point of view of socio-economically oriented interpretations. Moreover, the growth of the welfare sector in Hungary was not at its most rapid when industrialization and the related transformation of the employment structure progressed at its highest pace, i.e., in the 1950s and 1960s. The correlation between high economic growth and welfare policy was in fact negative during several high-growth periods: the greatest relative increase in welfare expenditures occurred when economic development slowed in the 1970s and 1980s.[11]

The ambiguous relationship between socio-economic development and welfare in East Central Europe is further demonstrated by demographic development. A decomposition analysis available for Hungary for the period between 1960 and 1989 shows that even though demographic factors contributed to the rise in pension expenditures, their influence was lagging far behind the consequences of the political decisions aiming at the expansion of social rights, similarly to Western Europe.[12] Moreover, the effects of demographic factors were peculiar in Hungary, where the negative demographic consequences of forced industrialization along with the promotion of women's employment led to a population policy that was much more proactive than in any West European country. The vigorous policy to boost the Hungarian birthrate was reflected in the relatively high number of family and maternity benefits, which far surpassed West European levels in the mid-1960s. Consequently, demographic factors in Hungary mediated the effects of not only economic but also political transformations to the welfare sector.

Political, rather than socio-economic, factors are dominant in the welfare development of East Central Europe. The nature of political factors diverged considerably from much of Western Europe, since political mobilization and class-alliance were not major determinants of welfare state formation in East Central European societies. During the communist era, class mobilization in the traditional sense was impossible because of the power monopoly of the state-party.[13] Instead, ideological factors shaped the communist welfare system.[14] Egalitarian claims appeared in the official ideology and propaganda, especially in the early decades: comprehensive social security was considered to be an inherent part of the society since it was meant to express the humanity of the communist system.

Nevertheless, such declarations did not mean that collectivist or egalitarian principles were the dominant. Other principles carried more weight than welfare and therefore competed with welfare policies, such as the practice of offering privileges to certain social strata that were regarded as pillars of communism or necessity of increasing economic output. Moreover, the collectivist ideology excluded those groups who were seen as "parasites" and "speculators" and were therefore excluded from welfare services. The fact that social security and other welfare benefits were distributed according to class was openly acknowledged: indeed, receiving welfare went hand in hand with work performance, discipline and productivity. Loyalty was also rewarded, for example, in the so-called "personal pensions."[15] In the early years, social security did not appear as a fundamental right of the citizens, but was seen as a gift from the state that reflected the government's benevolence.

In the interpretation of welfare development dynamics in communist Hungary, a considerable role must be attributed to political constraints, with which the system was confronted in different forms from time to time, such as the overt opposition of the population in 1956, or the eroding legitimacy of the regime in the late 1980s. In several West European countries, the prospect of parliamentary elections had the effect of increasing welfare benefits.[16] In Hungary, this type of electoral cycle was absent throughout the century. Instead, a kind of "crisis cycle" emerged: as early as the first half of the 20th century, there were signs that the increase of social benefits was related to political cataclysms. Immediately after the Second World War, coverage was increased, and the same happened in the years following the 1956 revolution. This pattern emerged again when we witnessed the highest social expenditures during the under extremely dire economic and political conditions in Hungary in the late 198s.[17]

As far as the other East Central European countries are concerned, the determinants of welfare development have only slightly diverged from the Hungarian case. Economic development and, in its wake, the changes in employment and demographic factors contributed to the long-term development of social security programs. However, the emergence of welfare programs, their timing and dynamics cannot be explained by the level of socio-economic development. Political factors, such as the legitimating efforts of the elites, the relative weakness of liberalism and national attempts to promote industrial development directly influenced the expansion of social security programs early on. During the inter-war period, class alliances to advance welfare legislation only existed in Czechoslovakia, where agricultural workers enjoyed a relatively high level of social security benefits. In Hungary and Poland, the political influence of Christian parties and the assertion of landowners' interests, carried greater weight than economic and social conditions in influencing social policies.[18]

After the Second World War, a pronounced convergence between the East Central European communist countries took place, enhanced by the diffusion of the Soviet political and economic system and the communist ideology. During the communist era, the cases of Czechoslovakia and Poland fully confirm the conclusions drawn from the Hungarian experience. The dynamics of the changes were less influenced by economic factors, but again to a much greater degree by political ones: the communist ideology with its inherent contradictions, political and economic crises, legitimating efforts and diffusion processes all worked to influence social welfare policies more than socio-economic factors.[19]

Based on the interplay between factors described above, a peculiar mix of welfare arrangements emerged in post-War East Central Europe, These welfare systems not only had specific communist characteristics, but also reflected features found in other—conservative and social democratic—regimes. Full-employment (in fact, compulsory or forced employment of the working-age population) was the basic institution of social welfare, even if it did not entirely succeed. Other important aspects of communist welfare included price subsidies for basic goods and services and the system of social benefits offered by companies (fringe benefits), though these benefits changed significantly over time and in different countries. In addition, the functions of social security changed in a peculiar and contradictory way in communist East Central Europe. On the one hand, the elimination of traditional institutions of poverty relief increased the relative significance of social security programs. On the other hand, the influence of social policy considerations in other areas, which enjoyed relative autonomy in Western European societies (such as price mechanisms or the labor market), reduced the importance of social security within the whole welfare system.[20]

That said, it is misleading to identify post-Second World War East Central European welfare regimes with the distinctive communist features of the system, because it also consisted of different elements of welfare arrangements prevalent in contemporary Western Europe. In addition to embracing communism, Hungary and the other countries in the region adopted the Bismarckian principles of social security at an early stage. Bismarckian traditions found their way into the new welfare systems of the communist countries since they were consistent with certain goals. In the 1950s, a differentiation of social security eligibility took place in Hungary, where industrial workers, the armed forces, party and state bureaucracy were privileged while the agricultural population was neglected.[21] Even more importantly, after a marked leveling off policy of the early communist years, there was a heavily work-related element in the benefit structure. Important social security services (cash benefits, such as pensions or sick pay) were tied to individual contributions, which was similar to the conservative or corporatist West European welfare systems.[22] The Bismarckian precedents of the social security system have clearly mitigated corporatist features, however, since the communist authorities were not shy about tinkering with welfare schemes by rescinding certain rights when they saw fit.[23] Tying benefits to work performance came from the communist ideology of placing high value on production and workforce mobilization. With time, this characteristic of the welfare policy became even more pronounced.

The crudest forms of discrimination were abolished in Hungary in the second half of the 1950s. The growing significance of the solidarity principle of the 1960s and 1970s in the area of qualifying conditions paired with the rapid increase of coverage can be regarded as a move toward universality—a major feature of social democratic welfare regimes. Thus, in Hungary the entire population was covered by social insurance sooner than in most West European countries. Of course, when compared to the West, the relative level of benefits in Hungary does not turn out so favorably, although the ratio of pensions relative to earnings corresponded to the Western average in the early 1980s. By the 1980s, an increasing number of benefits were based on Hungarian citizenship. By the mid 1970s, all in-kind benefits for health care were citizenship-based, similar to the British or Swedish systems. These similarities to different types of Western European welfare regimes suggest that by the 1980s, the Hungarian social insurance system applied a combination of elements customary in Western Europe as qualifying conditions.

During this period, the Hungarian welfare system reflected the simultaneous presence of the communist, social democratic and Bismarckian features. For example, the old age pension scheme had features of all three systems. Similarly to social democratic regimes, coverage was at a high level, administration was centralized with the state playing the central role in its organization. The specific rights given to individual social groups and the strong work- and income-relatedness of pensions are features of the conservative welfare systems. In fact, only the low relative significance of social security pensions within the welfare system in the 1980s—mainly due to the crowding out effect of price subsidies and fringe benefits—can be regarded as a communist characteristic of the pension scheme.

The decades after the Second World War saw an increased uniformity in the East Central European region in terms of welfare policy. Regional convergence manifests itself in the level of social security expenditure. Initially, Czechoslovakia had an exceptionally high social security expenditure/national income ratio: in 1965 the ratio was almost double of that in Poland and Hungary. But by 1980, these differences almost disappeared throughout the region.[24] The same is true regarding the gaps between the three East Central European countries in terms of social rights. Poland was an outlier initially, due to the high number of private farmers who were ineligible for pension insurance.[25] By the 1980s, however, disparities within the region decreased. In Hungary as well as in Czechoslovakia, the mid-1970s was the turning point, when universal coverage became the underlying concept in social security. In Poland this development took place somewhat later, at the end of the 1970s.[26]

East Central European welfare after 1990: Institutionalized volatility?

The transition to a market economy in the 1990s deeply challenged the East Central European welfare systems. Not only did it mean the end of major features of communist welfare, such as guaranteed employment and subsidized prices on basic necessities, but it also meant that the effort to make the social security compatible with a market economy shook the communist era welfare structure to its core. The challenges to the old system were great. First, the social costs of the transition increased demand for welfare services, while the number of contributors significantly decreased as a result of mass unemployment, the growing informal sector and the easy availability of early retirement and disability pensions. In Hungary, the first years of economic transition did not witness a significant decrease in social expenditures. In fact, spending increased since the government introduced costly programs—such as unemployment benefits and new social assistance schemes—in order to meet the social needs created by the emergence of mass unemployment and subsequent rise in poverty. Existing social security benefits remained unchanged for several years, although their real value had eroded substantially.[27] In the end, the welfare system retained its mixed character, although the communist features disappeared quickly and the mix of social democratic and conservative principles prevailed. These patterns were deeply rooted not only in institutions but also in public attitudes. According to polls, the majority of the electorate favored a combination of universal social welfare arrangements (especially in health care) and work-based benefits (cash benefits).[28]

Despite the considerable path-dependency in welfare institutions and high public support of a large-scale welfare state, liberal reforms challenged the status quo and led to a significant degree of volatility in the welfare system. 1995 marked a watershed in the Hungarian social welfare system when, as part of an austerity program, social benefits were cut substantially by the new ex-communist (socialist) government, with a promise of further cuts over following next years. In the first two years of the austerity program (in 1995 and 1996), the decrease in social expenditures equaled 5 percent of the GDP—a fall from 29.5 percent to 24.3 percent. The primary means of this retrenchment was the non-indexation of benefits, implemented at a time when inflation was galloping well over 20 percent annually. In addition to non-indexation, some entitlements were cut substantially.[29] Both of the two biggest cash welfare schemes—pension and family allowances—were affected by these reforms.

Another method used by the government to curtail social expenditures in 1995 was to raise the retirement age (55 for women and 60 for men) to a uniform 62 years. The new system was modeled after Latin-American (Chilean and Argentinean) precedents, which were favored by international agencies such as the IMF and the World Bank. The system was composed of three pillars: a basic state pension, a compulsory private pension, and a voluntary private pension. Joining the new pension scheme became compulsory for new entrants of social security, and optional for employees under 47. One-fourth of the total contribution of employers and insured persons was scheduled to go to the second pillar, that is, to private pension funds.[30] From 1995 to 1997, the universal family allowance was also abolished. A means-test procedure was introduced first for families with no more than two children, then for all families.[31]

All the same, there was no consensus about the direction of welfare reforms among the political elite. After the 1998 elections, the new conservative government abolished several aspects of the austerity program by reintroducing redistributive principles and universal entitlements. It revised the pension law and reset the contributions to private insurance companies at a lower level in order to raise public pension fund revenues. This step could only partly balance the introduction of private insurance schemes. Nevertheless, the pension system retained its predominantly public nature, and brought back almost universal coverage. The pensions are based on contributions, that is, on work performance. There is a redistributive element as well, since a modest vertical redistribution among contributors also takes place. This latter characteristic of the public pension system has even been strengthened during the transformation, since indexation was often applied to pensions in a non-linear way, which favored lower pensions. The ratio of private pension spending to total pension expenditure was almost negligible in Hungary in the 1990s. The new government reintroduced the universal rights based on citizenship for family allowance and maternity benefits. This meant the rehabilitation of the citizenship principle as a source of rights in the welfare system, which means-testing receded to the background.[32]

There is no indication of a liberal transformation in other major areas of welfare. Other social security schemes remained universal, the most important of which being the cash and in-kind benefits of health insurance, even if widespread corruption institutionalized under communism in that sector hinders the effective realization of social rights to a considerable extent. The role of means-tested poverty relief and other social assistance, often regarded as an indicator of a liberal regime, has remained subordinate in Hungary. The share of social assistance within social expenditures was well below the ratio of liberal regimes in Esping-Andersen's study— only 3.3 percent, as opposed to 18 percent in the USA and 16 percent in Canada in 1980.[33] In this respect, the Hungarian welfare system would not qualify as a liberal regime in the Esping-Andersenian sense. However moderate the liberal tendencies were, they undoubtedly further increased the mixed character of the Hungarian welfare regime.

The convergence of the communist welfare systems in East Central Europe ceased to persist after 1990. The transition of the individual countries in the region showed some unique features in terms of welfare reform. In Poland, shock therapy went in tandem with the slow transformation of the welfare system, while pension reform received relatively extensive support from the political elite—unlike in Hungary.[34] In the Czech Republic, liberal economic rhetoric prevailed alongside surprisingly strong subsidies for social security in the first half of the 1990s. There, the most profound reforms were made in the area of health care, where a system of competing public health insurance funds was established, while benefits based on the principle of citizenship and universalism remained intact.[35] What made Slovakia unique was the even slower pace of reform throughout the 1990s, although the momentum has increased up considerably in recent years.[36]

As a result, the differences between the welfare systems of the East Central European countries increased somewhat as compared to the 1980s.[37] Despite all the changes and differences, however, outside political agencies and observers were either disillusioned (IMF, World Bank) or satisfied (EU) by the realization that the fast, liberal transformation of the welfare systems in line with the US model, had not been carried out in the region. For example, regarding the reforms of the region's health care system, an EU publication declared that "all health care financing reforms are in the mainstream of Western European tradition."[38] This statement can be regarded as somewhat inconsistent, though, since, unlike the World Bank and the IMF, the EU did not actually influence the region in social policy issues or make any attempts to do so.[39]

Since popular attitudes have favored an extensive welfare state in the East Central European countries, even moderate liberal reforms and tendencies call for some clarification. In part, the liberal reforms can be explained by the pressures placed on the region by international agencies with liberal agendas (IMF, World Bank), and by real or perceived pressures coming from the global economy.[40] However, these are only partial explanations. Especially from the mid-1990s onward, the activity and influence of these institutions has declined considerably. Because of low labor costs, the region has benefited from the growing internationalization of the economy, which means that globalization cannot be considered to be a major explanatory variable.

I suggest an alternative explanation. Due to the lasting efforts of communist regimes to prevent the evolution of civil society and the persistence of traditional communities, a massive social decapitalization took place in Hungary and in other East Central European countries, constituting one of the most significant social and cultural inheritances of communism.[41] The low level of social capital is expressed in trust and group membership far lower in the former communist countries than in the West. In 1990, only 25 percent of the respondents in Hungary and 35 percent in Poland trusted their fellow citizens unconditionally. By contrast, the level of interpersonal trust was considerably higher in most West European countries: the level of respondents who trusted their fellow citizens amounted to 65 percent in Norway, 66 percent in Sweden and 44 percent in Great Britain. Only Austria and some South-European countries came close to or slightly below the Polish level.[42] This low trust may contribute to low levels of social solidarity and to the inability of people to cooperate effectively in groups. I believe that the resulting organizational weakness and decreasing influence of welfare recipients vis-à-vis other groups interested in the retrenchment of the welfare state—coupled with the mixed features of welfare institutions—is the key factor in explaining why external and internal pressures for the residualization of the welfare state can persistently challenge the welfare status quo since 1990, causing considerable volatility of the welfare structures.[43] At this stage of my research the claim cannot be verified further. As indicated above, the role of cultural factors in welfare state development can be regarded as an underresearched area but at the same time it is a promising direction of research with regard to Western Europe. As far as East Central Europe is concerned, further research needs to be carried out on individual countries that will offer a comparative analysis.

As indicated earlier, the social and political legacies of the communism supported the emergence of volatile welfare policies in several ways. The legacy of the mixed character of the communist welfare state supported volatile policies. Even more importantly, there has been no stable class alliance behind the welfare regimes. Instead less stable factors, such as the communist ideology or political crises, determined welfare arrangements. The volatility of policies has been institutionalized by the inconsistency of values and attitudes of the population. On the one hand, we can see the high popular acceptance of the states' welfare activities. On the other hand, among welfare recipients we find a low level of social capital, social capability, organizational strength and other factors instrumental in the development of an advanced welfare state in the late 20th century in Western Europe. As a consequence, they cannot act effectively enough in the political arena and cannot form effective class alliances, which is necessary to influence welfare policy.

Conclusions

In this paper, I examined the foundations and development of post-Second World War welfare systems in East Central Europe. I argued that the determinants of East Central European welfare have differed considerably from the factors of welfare state formation elsewhere, and that these peculiarities greatly contributed to the present "mixed" characteristics of the region's welfare sectors. In Western Europe, in addition to the impact of industrialization and the changing structure of population and labor force, and most eminently the political mobilization of agents favoring extensive welfare programs constituted the major factors behind the rise of social rights. Political mobilization relied not only on forming class alliances to be effective, as it is emphasized in mainstream research. There were also social and cultural preconditions. Specific cultural values, such as honesty, trust and obedience to the state authorities, associability or social capabilities boosting cooperation and effective collective action have also facilitated the development of comprehensive welfare states.

Although economic and demographic factors were present in a similar way in East Central Europe, the determinants of the communist welfare system diverged considerably from that pattern. There, the major determinants of social policy included the communist ideology—with all its internal incoherence—initiating both universalistic and work-related social rights. Legitimating efforts, as well as political and economic crises represented other important elements that affected the trajectory of welfare systems. By contrast, political mobilization played a minor role in the formation of East Central European welfare systems. I also claim that it is misleading to identify the communist welfare system with its distinctive communist features since it also consisted of different elements of welfare arrangements prevalent elsewhere in post-war Europe. In th 1990s, the distinctive communist features disappeared quite quickly during the transition and, as a result, the institutional legacy of communism was much more a mixed system of conservative and universalistic welfare arrangements.

These mixed features have already increased the possibility of unsteadiness of the welfare arrangements. In addition, and somewhat paradoxically, the heritage of communism supported the emergence of liberal tendencies in the welfare systems of the new democracies. True, these tendencies are quite ambiguous. On the one hand, despite the liberal scenarios proposed by many early observers, the liberal transformation of the welfare systems has not taken place anywhere in East Central Europe. On the other hand, the prevailing liberal language of welfare discourse and the liberal reorganization of some welfare schemes call for explanation in a region where liberalism has never been influential and where polls have shown that popular support for liberal reforms are minimal. The influence of international agencies in countries with partly high indebtedness is a more important factor, as are real or perceived pressures coming from globalization. However, they can only be partial explanations, especially from the mid-1990s on, as the activity and influence of these agencies decreased considerably since that time and because of low labor costs, the region is generally seen to have benefited from globalization. I propose an alternative interpretation for the existence of liberal tendencies also related to the foundations of East Central European welfare in earlier decades, that is, the legacies of communism. I suggest that weak social capital and organizational weakness of welfare recipients are the key factors that explain why external and internal pressures for the residualization of welfare states can persistently challenge the welfare status quo in postcommunist East Central Europe, despite the institutional inertia and popular preferences mainly facilitating social democratic and conservative welfare arrangements. In fact, due to the politics of communist regimes which hindered the evolution of civil society and the persistence of traditional communities, a massive social decapitalization took place in East Central Europe constituting one of the most significant social and cultural legacies of communism.

The role of cultural factors in welfare development, however, needs further exploration and constitutes and important agenda for comparative welfare research. There are several possible paths here. The study of cultural values influencing the support and acceptance of the welfare state may prove to be promising in the future. The cultural approach might also be useful to refine the class mobilization theory by establishing the cultural preconditions of successful class alliance and other forms of cooperation in the welfare arena.

As a result, the instability of the postcommunist welfare arrangements does not simply result from an assumed transition from the communist to the liberal welfare system. Rather, the volatility can be regarded as an "institutionalized" characteristic of East Central European welfare sectors and we can expect the persistence of instability in postcommunist welfare policies until the democratic political institutions function more smoothly and reflect public preferences more effectively. This also suggests the important role of civil society in creating the preconditions for successful and durable reforms. The major lessons for decision makers involved in welfare reforms in the region and in countries with similar conditions outside the region include the need for genuine consensus-seeking before and during the implementation of reforms to avoid excessive risks of reform fiascos caused by the institutionalized volatility of welfare systems and the high costs of such policy failures.

ENDNOTES:

1. Gosta Esping-Andersen, *The Three Worlds of Welfare Capitalism* (Princeton: Princeton University Press, 1990).

2. Bob Deacon, "Developments in East European Social Policy," In Catherine Jones, ed., *New Perspectives on the Welfare State in Europe* (London and New York: Routledge, 1993), 196.

3. Gosta Esping-Andersen, "After the Golden Age? Welfare State Dilemmas in a Global Economy." In Gosta Esping-Andersen, ed., *Welfare States in Transition: National Adaptations in Global Economies* (London: Sage, 1996). 1-31.; Zsuzsa Ferge, "Social Policy Regimes and Social Structure." In Zsuzsa Ferge and Jon Eivind Kolberg, eds., *Social Policy in a Changing Europe* (Frankfurt/M. and Boulder, Co.: Campus, 1992), 220.

4. Mátyás J. Kovács, "Approaching the EU and Reaching the US? Rival Narratives on Transforming Welfare Regimes in East-Central Europe," *West European Politics* 25: 2 (2002): 175-204.

5. The relevant literature is vast, including Bob Deacon, "Eastern European Welfare States: The Impact of the Politics of Globalization," *Journal of European Social Policy* 10:2 (2000): 146-161.; Zsuzsa Ferge, "Welfare and 'Ill-fare' Systems in Central-Eastern Europe," In Robert Sykes, Bruno Palier and Pauline M. Prior, eds., *Globalization and European Welfare States. Challenges and Change* (Houndmills/ Basingstoke: Palgrave, 2001), 127-152.; Guy Standing, "Social Protection in Central and Eastern Europe: A Tale of Slipping Anchors and Torn Safety Nets," In Esping-Andersen, ed., *Welfare States in Transition*, 225-255.; János Kornai et al., eds., *Reforming the state: fiscal and welfare reform in post-socialist countries* (Cambridge: Cambridge University Press, 2001).

6. Orsolya Lelkes, "A great leap towards liberalism? The Hungarian welfare state," *International Journal of Social Welfare* 9 (2000): 92-102.

7. Béla Tomka, "Wohlfahrtsstaatliche Entwicklung in Ostmitteleuropa und das europäische Sozialmodell, 1945-1990." In Hartmut Kaelble and Günter Schmid, eds., *Das europäische Sozialmodell. Auf dem Weg zum transnationalen Sozialstaat* (WZB-Jahrbuch 2004, Berlin: Sigma, 2004), 107-139.; Important research findings emphasizing the lack of full-scale liberal transformation: Ulrike Götting, *Transformation der Wohlfahrtsstaaten in Mittel- und Osteuropa. Eine Zwischenbilanz* (Opladen: Leske und Budrich, 1998), 261-284.; Deacon, "Eastern European welfare states: the impact of the politics of globalization," 151.

8. The term "welfare state" describes the institutions that protect citizens from the negative consequences of illness, accident, unemployment and ageing.

9. For a recent literature review, see Edwin Amenta, "What We Know about the Development of Social Policy: Comparative and Historical Research in Comparative and Historical Perspective," In James Mahoney and Dietrich Rueschmeyer, *Comparative Historical Analyis in the Social Sciences* (Cambridge: Cambridge University Press, 2003), 91-130.; Locus classicus of the functionalist approach: Harold L. Wilensky, *The Welfare State and Equality: Structural and Ideological Roots of Public Expenditures* (Berkeley: University of California Press, 1975).; Frederick Pryor, *Public Expenditures in Communist and Capitalist Nations* (Homewood, Ill.: Richard D. Irwin, 1968).; Gaston V. Rimlinger, *Welfare Policy and Industrialization in Europe, America, and Russia* (New York: Wiley, 1971).; For the functionalist approach also, see Harold L. Wilensky et al., *Comparative Social Policy. Theories, Methods, Findings* (Berkeley: University of California Press, 1985), 8.; For an antithesis of the functionalist interpretation, see Peter Baldwin, *The Politics of Social Solidarity* (Cambridge: Cambridge University Press, 1990), 288-299.; Jens Alber, *Vom Armenhaus zum Wohlfahrtsstaat* (Frankfurt/M.: Campus, 1987), 120-125.; Walter Korpi, "Social Policy and Distributional Conflict in the Capitalist Democracies," *West European Politics* 3:3 (1980): 296-316.; Michael Shalev, "The Social Democratic Model and Beyond," *Comparative Social Research* 6 (1983): 315-351.; Walter Korpi, *The Democratic Class Struggle* (London: Routledge, 1983).; For an attept at a synthesis, see Peter Flora and Jens Alber, "Modernization, democratization and the development of welfare states in Western Europe," In Flora and Heidenheimer, eds., *The Development of Welfare States*, 65-68.; For the role of bureacratic traditions, see Hugh Heclo, *Modern Social Politics in Britain and Sweden* (New Haven, CT.: Yale University Press, 1974).; For the role of Catholic forces in welfare development, see Harold L. Wilensky, "Leftism, Catholicism, and Democratic Corporatism: The Role of Political Parties in Recent Welfare State Development," In Flora and Heidenheimer, eds., *The Development of Welfare States*, 356-358, 368-370.; For the positive role of left wing parties in the development in health insurance in the OECD area between 1930 and 1980, see Walter Korpi, "Power, Politics, and State Autonomy in the Development of Social Citizenship: Social Rights during Sickness in Eighteen OECD Countries since 1930," *American Sociological Review* 54:3 (1989): 309-328.; For conservative welfare states more specifically, see Kees van Kersbergen, *Social Capitalism: A Study of Christian Democracy and the Welfare State* (London: Routledge, 1995).; For the significance of class-alliance, see Esping-Andersen, *The Three Worlds of Welfare Capitalism*, 31-33.;

10. John Baldock, "Culture: The Missing Variable in Understanding Social Policy?" *Social Policy and Administration* 33:4 (1999): 458-473.; Carsten G. Ullrich, *Wohlfahrtsstaat und Wohlfahrtskultur* (Working Papers, Nr. 67. Mannheimer Zentrum für Europäische Sozialforschung. 2003).; Aage B. Sörensen, "On Kings, Pietism and Rent-seeking in Scandinavian Welfare States," *Acta Sociologica* 41:4 (1988): 363-375.; Wilensky, "Leftism, Catholicism and Democratic Corporatism."; Carsten G. Ullrich, "Die soziale Akzeptanz des Wohlfahrtsstaates," *Soziale Welt* 51 (2000): 131-151.; Christine S. Lipsmeyer and Timothy Nordstrom,

"East versus West: comparing political attitudes and welfare preferences across European societies," *Journal of European Public Policy* 10:3 (2003): 339-364.

11. Béla Tomka, *Szociálpolitika a 20. századi Magyarországon európai összehasonlításban* (Budapest: Századvég, 2003).

12. The increase in pension expenditures was primarily (60.4%) due to the increase in the ratio of those covered. A significantly lower contribution to the rise in pension expenditures, 22.4% came from the average increase of pension levels relative to the per capita economic output. An even smaller weight can be attributed to the growth of the pensioner-aged population (16.7%), while the change in the ratio of the active and inactive population effected only 0.5% of the increase. See Rudolf Andorka and István György Tóth, "A szociális kiadások és a szociálpolitika Magyarországon," In Rudolf Andorka, Tamás Kolosi and György Vukovich, eds., *Társadalmi riport, 1992* (Budapest: TÁRKI, 1992), 412-413.

13. Béla Tomka, *Welfare in East and West: Hungarian Social Security in an International Comparison, 1918-1990* (Berlin: Akademie Verlag, 2004), 105-111.

14. For the origins of communist social securtiy ideology, see Gaston V. Rimlinger, *Welfare Policy and Industrialization in Europe, America, and Russia* (New York: Wiley, 1971), 245-301.

15. Jiri Král and Martin Mácha, "Transforming of the old-age security in the Czech Republic," In Winfried Schmähl and Sabine Horstmann, eds., *Transformation of Pension Systems in Central and Eastern Europe* (Cheltenham: Edward Elgar, 2002), 224.

16. Maurizio Ferrera, "Italy." In Peter Flora, ed., *Growth to Limits. The Western European Welfare States Since World War II*. Vol. 2 (Berlin: de Gruyter, 1986), 446.

17. Andorka and Tóth, "A szociális kiadások és a szociálpolitika," 396-507.

18. For the social policy of Czechoslovakia and Poland in the interwar period, see ILO, *Compulsory Sickness Insurance. Studies and Reports, Series M, No. 6.* (Geneva: ILO, 1927), 217-219, 241-243.; ILO, *Compulsory Pension Insurance. Studies and Reports, Series M, No. 10.* (Geneva: ILO, 1933), 257-268, 331-341.; ILO, *International Survey of Social Sevice. Studies and Reports, Series M, No. 11.* (Geneva: ILO, 1933), 117-153, 511-545.

19. Tomka, "Wohlfahrtsstaatliche Entwicklung," 107-139.

20. For the communist welfare system, see Bob Deacon, *Social policy and socialism. The struggle for socialist relations of welfare* (London: Pluto Press, 1983).; John Dixon and David Macarov, eds., *Social welfare in socialist countries* (London and New York: Routledge, 1992).; Mojca Novak, "Reconsidering the socialist welfare state model," In Alison Woodward and Martin Kohli, eds., *Inclusions and Exclusions in European Societie* (London and New York: Routledge, 2001), 111-126.

21. Johan Jeroen De Deken, *Social Policy in Postwar Czechoslovakia* (EUI Working Paper SPS No. 1994/13. Florence: EUI, 1994), 137.

22. Endre Sik and Ivan Svetlik, "Similarities and Differences," In Adalbert Evens and H. Wintersberger, eds., *Shifts in the Welfare-Mix* (Frankfurt/M.: Campus, 1990), 276.

23. Jack Minkoff and Lynn Turgeon, "Income Maintanence in the Soviet Union in Eastern and Western Perspective." In Irving Louis Horowitz, ed., *Equity, Income and Policy* (New York and London: Praeger, 1977), 178–180.

24. Castles, "Whatever Happened to the Communist Welfare State," 217.

25. Maciej Zukowski, "Pensions Policy in Poland after 1945," In John Hills, John Ditch and Howard Glennerster, eds., *Beveridge and Social Security. An International Retrospective* (Oxford: Clarendon Press, 1994), 154–170.

26. Wlodzimierz Okrasa, "Social Welfare in Poland." In Julian Le Grand and Wlodzimierz Okrasa, eds., *Social Welfare in Britain and Poland* (London: STICERD, 1987), 14.

27. Zsuzsa Ferge and Katalin Tausz, "Social Security in Hungary: A Balance Sheet after Twelve Years," *Social Policy and Administration* 36 (2002): 178-195.

28. Zsuzsa Ferge, "Welfare and 'Ill-fare' Systems in Central-Eastern Europe," 151.

29. Lelkes, "A great leap towards liberalism," 94.

30. Béla Janky, *A magánnyugdíj-pénztárak tagsága* (TÁRKI Társadalompolitikai Tanulmányok. 18. Budapest: TÁRKI, 2000).

31. Michael F. Förster and István György Tóth, *Családi támogatások és gyermekszegénység a kilencvenes években Csehországban, Magyarországon és Lengyelországban* (TÁRKI Társadalompolitikai Tanulmányok 16. Budapest: TÁRKI, 1999), 26.; András Gábos, "Családok helyzete és családtámogatások a kilencvenes években," In Tamás Kolosi, István György Tóth and György Vukovich, eds., *Társadalmi Riport 2000* (Budapest: TÁRKI, 2000), 107–112.

32. Gábos, "Családok helyzete és családtámogatások a kilencvenes években," 112-113.

33. Lelkes, "A great leap towards liberalism," 101–102.

34. Tomasz Inglot, "Historical Legacies, Institutions, and the Politics of Social Policy in Hungary and Poland, 1989-1999," In Grzegorz Ekiert and Stephen E. Hanson, eds., *Capitalism and Democracy in Central and Eastern Europe. Assessing the Legacy of Communist Rule* (Cambridge: Cambridge University Press, 2003), 243.

35. Bob Deacon, "Eastern European welfare states: the impact of the politics of globalization," *Journal of European Social Policy* 10:2 (2000): 151.

36. Margita Hurcíková and Karol Pekník, "Transformation of old-age security in the Slovak Republic," In Schmähl and Horstmann, eds., *Transformation of Pension Systems in Central and Eastern Europe*, 249-276.

37. Katharina Müller, "From the State to the Market? Pension Reform Paths in Central-Eastern Europe and the Former Soviet Union," *Social Policy and Administration* 36:2 (2002): 159.

38. *Consensus Programme. Recent Reforms in Organisation, Financing and Delivery of Health Care in Central and Eastern Europe in Light of Accession to the European Union* (Conference May 1998. Brussels: European Commission, 1998).

39. Ulrike Götting, *Transformation der Wohlfahrtsstaaten in Mittel- und Osteuropa. Eine Zwischenbilanz* (Opladen: Leske und Budrich, 1998), 261-284.; Deacon, "Eastern European welfare states: the impact of the politics of globalization," 151.

40. Sabine Horstmann and Winfried Schmähl, "Explaining Reforms," In Schmähl and Horstmann, eds., *Transformation of Pension Systems in Central and Eastern Europe*, 63-81.

41. For social capital in East Central Europe, see Adam B: Seligman and Katalin Füzér, "The Problem of trust and the transition from state socialism," *Comparative Social Research* 14 (1994): 193-221.; Jan Delhey and Kenneth Newton, "Who trusts? The origins of social trust in seven societies," *European Societies* 5 (2003); Eric M. Uslaner, "Trust and civic engagement in East and West," In Gabriel Badescu and Eric M. Uslaner, eds., *Social Capital and the Transition to Democracy* (London and New York, 2003), 81-94.

42. Oscar W. Gabriel et al., *Sozialkapital und Demokratie. Zivilgesellschaftliche Ressourcen im Vergleich* (Wien: WUV Universitätsverlag, 2002), 58.

43. Claus Offe, "The politics of social policy in Eastern European transition: antecedents, agents, and agenda of reform," *Social Research* 60:4 (1993): 649-685.

THE NEW PENSION REFORMS: LESSONS FOR POST-SOVIET REPUBLICS

MITCHELL A. ORENSTEIN

N ew pension reforms involving the establishment of mandatory, private, individual pension savings accounts have revolutionized welfare state practices in a growing number of countries around the world, including in Central and Eastern Europe and some of the former Soviet republics, such as Estonia, Kazakhstan, Latvia, Lithuania and Russia. The new pension reforms overturn many of the core premises of traditional social security type pension systems that have dominated state social policy since World War II. These reforms are part of a broader neoliberal agenda of economic reform that has swept the world since first being enacted in Chile and Britain in the 1970s and 1980s.[1] They are significant because: (1) they radically alter the social contract and are thus highly controversial; (2) they represent a large proportion of the total economy; and, (3) they have been implemented through a global policy process with the direct involvement of global policy actors. This chapter briefly introduces the new pension reforms and explores the conditions for the implementation of such reforms in post-Soviet countries.

THE NEW PENSION REFORMS

The basic difference between social security and new pension reform systems can be summed up in a phrase: individual, private pension savings accounts. The new pension reforms introduce such accounts and seek to increase reliance on them as a means to fund retirement benefits over time. Of course, the nature and implications of these reforms are more complex. Social security and new pension reform systems are financed differently, administered differently, calculate and pay benefits differently, allocate risk differently and have different implications for labor markets, coverage rates and the economy as a whole.

Traditional social security pension systems in most countries of the world today are based on six principles:

1. *The state and/or employers* administer collections and benefits;
2. *Financing is 'pay-as-you-go,'* where current payroll tax revenues are used to pay current beneficiaries;
3. *Benefits are defined in advance and predictable* with clear expectations of retirement benefit level.
4. *Benefits may be redistributive* within and between generations and oriented towards preventing poverty;
5. *Benefits may be linked to lifetime income* to support a retirement consistent with a retiree's previous lifestyle;
6. *Risk is pooled* to provide social security against a variety of risks, including lacking old age income, disability and survivorship.

By contrast, the new pension reforms depend in part on mandatory savings in privately managed individual accounts. Private pension savings systems have the following features:

1. *The private sector administers* individual pension savings accounts in a manner similar to mutual funds.
2. *Financing is 'pre-funded,'* with pension benefits paid from funds collected ahead of time and invested in private accounts;
3. *Benefits are not defined in advance,* but depend upon investment returns and fees in private accounts;
4. *Benefits are linked strictly to past contributions;*
5. *There is little or no redistribution* within or between generations, though other redistributive mechanisms may be preserved or created;
6. *Risk and reward is individualized,* with individuals taking greater risk for their own retirement, but potentially realizing greater returns as well.

Social security and new pension reform systems both require mandatory payroll tax contributions and both provide state-mandated savings for old age security. However, they do so in very different ways with very different economic consequences, reflecting different philosophies of welfare state provision. Social security systems are an outgrowth of

European traditions of state social provision. They emphasize solidarity of citizens within the nation state. New pension reform systems emphasize individual saving, individual responsibility and incentives, choice and returns. While both social security and new pension reform systems rely on payroll tax revenue, they differ in the use of these payroll taxes. In social security systems, current payroll tax contributions are used to pay current beneficiaries. This type of financing is called 'pay-as-you-go.' New pension reform systems are pre-funded. Individuals deposit contributions in their private pension savings accounts during their working life and draw on these contributions—to which investment returns are added and management fees are subtracted—after retirement.

Figure 1: Financing of pension systems

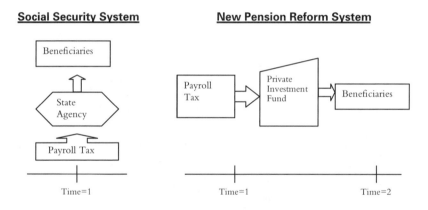

REPLACEMENT, PARALLEL AND MIXED REFORMS

In most countries that have adopted pension reforms, the traditional social security system has been maintained in part or in whole. Müller shows that there are three types of new pension reform systems: substitutive, parallel and mixed.[2] In substitutive reforms, the former state social security system is completely replaced by one based on private, individual accounts. In mixed reforms, a system of private, individual accounts is established along side a reduced state social security system. In parallel reforms, the two systems exist side by side and people can choose which system to join. In Table 1, the 25 countries that had adopted new pension reforms including savings in private, funded accounts by 2004 are categorized by type of reform and are listed in each category by date.

Table 1: Types of New Pension Reforms[3]

Substitutive	Mixed	Parallel
Chile 1981	Sweden 1994	Peru 1993
Bolivia 1997	Argentina 1994	Colombia 1994
Mexico 1997	Uruguay 1996	Estonia 2001
El Salvador 1998	Hungary 1998	Lithuania 2002
Kazakhstan 1998	Poland 1999	
Dom. Rep. 2001	Costa Rica 2001	
Nicaragua 2001	Latvia 2001	
Kosovo 2001	Bulgaria 2002	
	Croatia 2002	
	Macedonia 2002	
	Russia 2002	
	Slovakia 2003	

REFORM IN THE POST-SOVIET STATES

From Table 1, it is apparent that many of the Central and East European (CEE)countries that were or are involved in the European Union accession process, such as Hungary, Poland, Slovakia, Latvia, Lithuania, Estonia, Bulgaria and Croatia, have reformed their pension systems. Kazakhstan and Russia are the only two former Soviet Union (FSU) states to have launched these reforms, outside of the Baltic States. On the one hand, the popularity of these reforms in Central and Eastern Europe suggests that the new pension reforms may also provide a way forward for reform in poorer former Soviet Republics. On the other hand, conditions in the poorer former Soviet Republics may be different enough that the new pension reforms may not be appropriate. The following sections analyze differences between CEE and FSU states and present an analysis of how the new pension reforms may need to be tailored to fit specific conditions in the post-Soviet countries.

Pension systems in poorer post-Soviet countries differ in many ways from those of the CEE states. In countries with higher poverty rates, lower pension system coverage, poorer administration, average benefits that fall below an absolute poverty line of $2.00 per day, and smaller pension systems serving younger populations, the right reform strategy may be different from that applied in richer countries with aging populations and mature pension systems imposing enormous fiscal burdens. In particular, major improvements are needed in increasing pension system coverage and benefit adequacy.

PENSION SYSTEM CHALLENGES

The last decade has seen 11 postcommunist countries adopt the new pension reforms—nine in Central and Eastern Europe, plus Russia and Kazakhstan. Transnational actors have played a significant role in facilitating these changes, as part of a broad coalition including the World Bank Social Protection division, USAID, OECD and other organizations. However, as these organizations turn their attention further east to the less developed countries of the former Soviet Union, the pension system challenges and opportunities in these countries are far different from those encountered in CEE.

Major differences include:

1. **Higher Poverty**: Pension systems play a role in preventing poverty everywhere, but the anti-poverty dimension of pension systems is particularly important in countries with very high poverty rates.
2. **Less Functional States**: Less developed postcommunist states also have limited state capacity, resulting in a deeper crisis in pension system administration. This is reflected in low and more steeply declining rates of coverage for pension systems.
3. **Less Mature Pension Systems**: Less developed former communist countries also tend to be younger, with less mature and smaller pension systems, and therefore do not face the same fiscal challenges that have made multi-pillar reform so critical in CEE.
4. **Greater Threat from Alternative Providers**: As pension systems have decayed in many former communist countries, a host of alternative social service providers have emerged, some of which may threaten state and international security.

Pensions and Poverty

Postcommunist less developed countries (LDCs) have extraordinarily high poverty rates. From a global perspective, what is particularly notable is not the absolute levels of poverty in these countries, but the rapid spread of poverty since 1989. The postcommunist LDCs stand out as the most steeply declining set of countries in terms of broad social welfare and human development, at a time when most other parts of the world—including large developing countries such as India and China—enjoy growth that lifts both rich and poor.

In this context, the poverty reduction dimension of pension systems is all the more important. It is more important because a higher percentage of pensioners live in poverty, because cash incomes from pension benefits help to lift a larger proportion of people out of poverty, and because a greater proportion of pensioners are likely to receive benefits near to the statutory minimum. This implies that issues of pension system coverage and minimum pension benefits are far more important than in leading European Union accession countries.

Failed Welfare States

While need is greater in the postcommunist LDCs, state capacity to provide for social needs is in steep decline, even in collapse. Under communism, governments provided low but adequate pension benefits to nearly everyone. But the Western-oriented market transition has caused governments to renege on these promises. Postcommunist LDCs today provide average pension benefits that, in many cases, lie below an absolute poverty line of $2.00 per day in 2000 dollars. Some even provide benefits that amount to less than $1.00 per day. In comparison to CEE EU accession states, all of which provide average pension benefits above absolute poverty lines, in postcommunist LDCs, much greater attention needs to be paid to issues of pension adequacy.

Table 1 shows that nearly half of postcommunist European and Eurasian countries pay average pension benefits below $2.00 per day. Four paid average pension benefits that fell below a $1.00 per day absolute poverty line in 2002 are: Ukraine, Azerbaijan, Moldova, and Armenia. Ukraine subsequently raised its benefits in 2003 to an average payment of $27.90 per month in 2000 dollars. Only two prospective European Union members fell below the $2.00 a day level—Romania and Bulgaria.

Table 2: Average Pension Benefit (USD/ month in 2000 dollars), 2002

Rank	Country	Average Pension Benefit
1	Slovenia	743.37
2	Croatia	209.51
3	Poland	208.53
4	Czech Republic	166.30
5	Hungary (2001)	129.19
6	Slovakia	107.86
7	Latvia	101.39
8	Estonia	94.79
9	Georgia	87.59★
10	Lithuania	79.72
11	Macedonia	65.11
12	Bulgaria	42.99
13	Albania	40.37
14	Belarus	37.56
15	Romania	36.60
16	Russia	36.27
17	Kazakhstan	35.69
18	Ukraine	21.42
19	Azerbaijan	11.67
20	Moldova	10.54
21	Armenia	10.22

Source: USAID. European Union accession states italicized.

★ Data uncertain for Georgia.

Inadequate pensions are influenced by two main factors: economic development and state capacity. Part of pension inadequacy in the post-communist LDCs of course results from poor economic performance. However, even correcting for economic performance, postcommunist LDCs still spend less on pensions than their CEE neighbors. This can be seen by looking at the ratio of average pensions to average wages in the new USAID dataset. CEE accession countries not only have higher wage rates, but they devote a greater share of average wages to pension provision. All current CEE EU accession states pay an average pension that exceeds 30 percent of the average wage. Most postcommunist countries provide an average pension benefit of between 30 and 50 percent of the average wage. However, five countries fall below this measure of pension adequacy: Kazakhstan, Romania, Moldova, Macedonia and Armenia.

Table 3: Ratio of Average Pension to Average Wage, 2002

Rank	Country	Replacement Ratio
1	Georgia (2001)	1.51*
2	Slovenia	1.30
3	Azerbaijan	0.56
4	Latvia	0.52
5	Czech Republic (2001)	0.46
6	Ukraine	0.42
7	Belarus	0.40
8	Albania (2001)	0.40
9	Bulgaria	0.40
10	Hungary (2001)	0.38
11	Slovakia	0.38
12	Poland	0.38
13	Croatia	0.34
14	Russia	0.32
15	Lithuania	0.32
16	Estonia	0.31
17	Kazakhstan	0.29
18	Moldova (2003)	0.27
19	Romania (2003)	0.23
20	Macedonia (2000)	0.12
21	Armenia (2001)	0.11

Source: USAID. European Union accession states italicized.
* Data for Georgia may be unreliable.

An even greater problem than average pension adequacy is pension system coverage. Here the differences between CEE accession states and postcommunist LDCs are most stark. Coverage rates are measured here as the proportion of the labor force contributing to the pension system (and therefore receiving benefits after retirement). Central European EU accession states still have 60 to 86 percent of the labor force contributing to the pension system, nearing OECD levels in many cases. However, coverage rates for other former communist countries have declined precipitously in recent years, falling from near 100 percent to less than 50 percent in many cases. Most postcommunist LDCs cover less than two-thirds of the workforce. And since higher income workers are more likely to pay into the system and receive benefits, we can assume that many of the poorest are not being reached. Coverage rates in many post-communist LDCs are still higher than in much of the developing world, where coverage is often limited to 10 to 30 percent of the workforce, but several countries appear to have fallen to third-world levels.

Table 4: Pension Coverage Rates (Percent of Labor Force Contributing, mid-1990s)

Rank	Country	Coverage Rate
1	Belarus	97.0
2	Slovenia	86.0
3	Czech Republic	85.0
4	Hungary	77.0
5	Estonia	76.0
6	Lithuania	74.3
7	Slovakia	73.0
8	Ukraine	69.8
9	Poland	68.0
10	Armenia	66.6
11	Croatia	66.0
12	Latvia	60.5
13	Romania	55.0
14	Azerbaijan	52.0
15	Kazakhstan	51.0
16	Macedonia	49.0
17	Kyrgyzstan	44.0
18	Georgia	41.7
19	Moldova	34.5
20	Albania	32.0

Source: Müller 2003 based on World Bank and ILO.

In conclusion, whereas pension systems in Central European EU accession countries constitute an effective bulwark against poverty, those in postcommunist LDCs do not. Central European accession countries provide average pension benefits that exceed 30 percent of the average wage and a $2.00 per day absolute poverty line and reach the vast majority of the labor force. Pension systems in many postcommunist LDCs face greater challenges in terms of pension adequacy and coverage. Average pensions provide benefits that fall below absolute poverty lines and cover less than half the workforce in many cases. Part of the problem is economic development, but part is linked to lower state capacity, as reflected in low coverage rates and lower average pension to average wage replacement ratios. Post-communist LDCs simply do not or cannot carry out welfare state functions as well as their CEE neighbors, despite the strong legacy of communist era social protection that still sets these countries apart from much of the developing world.

POST-SOVIET PENSION SYSTEMS COMPARED

While the previous section has drawn general distinctions between CEE and FSU pension systems, there is substantial variation in the extent and nature of post-Soviet pension system vulnerability. Based on the three criteria identified above, low benefits, low replacement rates, and low coverage, seven former Soviet and CEE countries can be judged to be highly vulnerable. These include Albania, Moldova, Georgia, Kyrgyzstan, Macedonia, Kazakhstan, Azerbaijan and Romania. In these countries, coverage rates range from 31 to 55 percent, below the level of the lowest current CEE EU accession states.

Five states are highly vulnerable in terms of having average pension replacement rates of less than 30 percent of average wage: Armenia, Macedonia, Romania, Moldova and Kazakhstan. Armenia, Moldova, Azerbaijan, and Ukraine are vulnerable for having average pension benefits below the absolute poverty line of $1.00 per day.

If one defines the most vulnerable pension systems as those that are highly vulnerable in two of the three key indicators of pension system vulnerability, six may be judged most vulnerable: Armenia, Azerbaijan, Moldova, Macedonia, Romania and Kazakhstan. Albania, Georgia and Kyrgyzstan are of special concern because of low coverage rates. In addition, we lack data for some additional countries. Failure to produce data may correlate with low state capacity. However, states for which no data is available by definition cannot be judged to be among the most vulnerable systems. Nonetheless, they are noted on Table 4.

Table 5: Most Vulnerable Pension Systems

	1. Low Benefits	2. Low Replacement Rates	3. Low Coverage	4. No Data	Total Vulnerability (Sum of 1-4)
Albania			●		●
Armenia	●	●			●●
Azerbaijan	●		●		●●
Bosnia				○	¤
Georgia			●		●
Kazakhstan	●		●		●●
Kosovo				○	○
Kyrgyzstan			●		●
Macedonia		●	●		●●
Moldova	●	●	●		●●●
Romania		●	●		●●
Serbia				○	○
Tajikistan				○	○
Turkmenistan				○	○
Ukraine	●				●
Uzbekistan				○	○

RETHINKING THE STRATEGY

To date, most international pension assistance has emphasized structural reform towards multi-pillar pension systems. While there are a host of excellent reasons to continue to support such reform, it must be recognized that the rationale for pursuing such reforms is diminished in many postcommunist LDCs. Multi-pillar reforms make greater sense in countries with large, un-funded pension commitments, as in the OECD and CEE EU accession states. Countries with smaller, less generous and less extensive pension obligations may not need pension privatization as much. Likewise, countries with younger demographic profiles do not face the same type of social security shortfalls. In these countries, administrative strengthening measures to increase coverage rates and benefit adequacy may be more important.

Such an approach also would be consistent with the approach towards pension policy advice taken by the World Bank since 1994. While the World Bank has pursued multi-pillar reform in relatively more developed countries, it has simultaneously encouraged LDCs to undertake programs of administrative strengthening prior to initiating multi-pillar reform.

LESSONS FOR POST-SOVIET STATES

During the process of spreading the new pension reforms, thinking has continued to evolve within the major international organizations in this area. In particular, visible debates have taken place within the World Bank that provide important lessons for post-Soviet states considering the new pension reforms. In 1999, then World Bank Chief Economist Joseph Stiglitz began to question the World Bank's approach to pension reform. In his essay, "Ten Myths of Pension Reform," Stiglitz suggested that the Bank needed to take a wider view of the possibilities of pension reform and not advocate a single, narrow model.[4] Secondly, a World Bank book by Gill, Packard and Yermo raised serious questions about some of the disadvantages of multipillar pension reforms in Latin America, particularly from the point of view of high administrative fees, low participation rates and other inefficiencies.[5] Barr advocated substantially curtailing Bank support for multipillar pension systems.[6]

Holzmann and Hinz responded to some of the challenges voiced in the World Bank by amending and updating the pension reform model proposed in *Averting*.[7] In particular, Holzmann and Hinz advocate greater flexibility in designing pension systems in accordance with particular country situations and preferences. Secondly, they advocate the establishment of a "zero" pillar of noncontributory benefits to reduce poverty and improve the overall coverage rates of pension systems in developing countries. Finally, Holzmann and Hinz discuss an array of administrative improvements and design lessons from experience that can be implemented in further reforming countries

Several of these lessons are particularly relevant to post–Soviet states. In many former Soviet republics, coverage rates of pension systems have collapsed from near 100 percent to below 50 percent. Most people simply are not contributing to pension systems, either because they are unemployed or employed in the informal sector. Therefore, any system that pays benefits only to those in the formal sector will fail to pay pensions to a majority of the population and will most probably end up securing the privilege of relatively well-off earners versus the neediest segment of the population. Post-Soviet states may wish to pay greater attention to the design of non-contributory minimum pension standards in order to provide higher pension coverage and to prevent poverty.

Second, experience has shown that administration of mandatory, private pension systems is highly complex. Developing countries may not have the regulatory infrastructure to support such systems. Building such infrastructure can involve years, if not decades, of reliance on global policy actors for implementation assistance and possible losses for pension system participants. It may be prudent to wait until administrative and regulatory frameworks are in place before implementing such reforms.

CONCLUSIONS

This chapter has explored the nature of the new pension reforms and shown that they have been spread by a transnational advocacy coalition made up of international organizations and other global policy actors. These actors have had a large role in the development, transfer and implementation of the new pension reforms in 25 countries around the world. Global experience with the new pension reforms also provides some lessons for post-Soviet states, namely to give sufficient priority to the design of "zero pillar" noncontributory pensions and administrative and regulatory complexity of systems based on private, mandatory individual savings accounts. Making use of these lessons will allow post-Soviet states to draw on the latest technology of pension system design while also addressing local conditions, including high poverty and low state and private sector regulatory capacity.

ENDNOTES

1. Campbell, John L. and Ove K. Pedersen, eds., *The Rise of Neoliberalism and Institutional Analysis* (Princeton: Princeton University Press, 2001).
2. Müller, Katharina, *Privatising Old-Age Security: Latin America and Eastern Europe Compared,* (Aldershot, UK: Edward Elgar, 2003).

3. Sources: Orenstein 2000; Madrid 2003; Müller *Privatising Old-Age Security*; Fultz, *Recent Trends;* Palacios 2003; and web resources from World Bank, IDB, and USAID.

4. Orszag, Peter R. and Joseph E. Stiglitz, "Rethinking Pension Reform: Ten Myths about Social Security Systems," In Holzmann and Stiglitz, eds., *New Ideas about Old Age Security.*

5. Gill, Indermit S., Truman Packard and Juan Yermo, *Keeping the Promise of Social Security in Latin America,* (Washington, DC: Stanford University Press and The World Bank, 2005).

6. Barr, Nicholas, ed., *Labor Markets and Social Policy in Central and Eastern Europe,* (Washington, DC: The World Bank, 2005).

7. Holzmann, Robert and Richard Hinz, *Old Age Income Support in the 21ˢᵗ Century,* (Washington, DC: The World Bank, 2005).

WELFARE STATES, CONSTITUENCIES AND POSTCOMMUNIST TRANSITIONS

LINDA J. COOK

The conference on *Fighting Poverty and Reforming Social Security* addressed the question: What lessons can post-soviet states learn from the new democracies of Central Europe? It began with the observation that most Central European democracies have succeeded in introducing institutional welfare state reforms, and in adapting their social security systems to address poverty and other transitional social problems. Most post-soviet states, by contrast, still do not provide modernized, reliable welfare protection to their citizens. This paper argues that domestic political-institutional differences were a key factor in producing these divergent outcomes. In Central European states, democratic bargaining over welfare reform contributed to more modest retrenchment and more gradual restructuring. In the authoritarian and semi-authoritarian post-soviet context, welfare states were either radically liberalized by executives or retained as statist bureaucracies. My study relies on evidence from five postcommunist cases, the Central European states of Poland and Hungary and the post-soviet states of Russia, Belarus and Kazakhstan, to illustrate and explain these patterns of change. The major lesson it draws from Central Europe is that welfare improvements are likely to come to the post-soviet states with democratization.

All postcommunist states went through periods of welfare state retrenchment and programmatic liberalization during the 1990s. Faced with economic recessions and new problems of poverty and unemployment, governments reduced subsidies and entitlements, introduced means-testing of benefits to direct them toward the new poor, and privatized some welfare services. But the scope and consequences of these changes varied across the postcommunist space. In Poland and Hungary, welfare effort (i.e., spending as percent of GDP) was generally sustained, institutional change was relatively effective and the state retained a strong commitment to social provision. In the post-soviet states of Russia and Kazakhstan, by contrast, welfare policy was marked by radical change, failed institutional reforms and the severe decay in the states' welfare functions. In Belarus, welfare effort was sustained but was used to maintain a centralized welfare bureaucracy that did not adapt to changing societal needs.

I argue that politics was a central factor in accounting for these differences. This argument begins with the claim that all welfare states produce constituencies. These constituencies include groups that benefit from social spending and programs as recipients, public sector workers or state-based administrators of the social welfare services.[1] Because communist states featured comprehensive, low-provisioned welfare states, such constituencies were strongly present in postcommunist states as well. Postcommunist welfare constituencies took two main forms: as latent societal interest groups that worked in or received services and benefits from the welfare state, and as state-bureaucratic actors who depended on public expenditure and administration of inherited social sectors. In the democratic states of Central Europe, societal constituencies of benefit recipients and public sector workers gained some representation through social-democratic parties, trade unions and professional associations. Electoral accountability and other political mechanisms allowed them to influence welfare policy. These constituencies had much less influence than their counterparts in advanced industrial democracies because of the relative weakness of representative institutions in Central Europe, but they still played a role in welfare policy-making.

In post-soviet states, by contrast, societal constituencies generally lacked or had very weak political rights or influence on policy change. Here, defense of the welfare state depended mainly on state-bureaucratic actors. In some cases (Russia in the early 1990s and Kazakhstan throughout) both societal and statist welfare constituencies lacked influence. In these cases, executive liberalizers were able to cut expenditures and carry out rapid, largely unconstrained institutional change. As evidence from Russia and Kazakhstan will show, these policy reforms usually failed to provide substitutes for the statist welfare structures they were supposed to replace, leading instead to break-downs and lapses in welfare provision. They are examples of what Guillermo O'Donnell calls 'low-quality' policy, implemented rapidly by executive authorities with little bargaining, consultation or understanding of institutional contexts. Such policies were not absent in Central Europe—Hungary's early health sector reforms were nearly as ill conceived—but they were exceptional. In Central Europe, democratic mechanisms generally assured that institutional changes were more gradual and bargained, producing better-quality and more effective policy outcomes.

Where statist actors were strong in the post-soviet context, they did defend welfare claims. Here, Belarus provides a clear example.[2] State bureaucracies retained much of their power in the Belarussian polity, and they sustained levels of welfare effort to a greater extent than in the other post-soviet cases. But these same interests also opposed liberalizing institutional reforms, and re-allocation of expenditures to the transitional needy. As a consequence, welfare provision remained centralized, bureaucratic and inefficient, and levels of poverty remained much higher than in Central Europe well into economic recovery. In the absence of pressures to make the welfare state responsive to societal needs, bureaucracies defended their own interests in institutional continuity.

In sum, authoritarian and semi-authoritarian post-soviet polities proved much less effective than Central European democracies in either preserving welfare effort or adapting welfare institutions to transitional needs. Democratic institutions—even the new and weak democratic institutions that were present in Poland and Hungary—helped make governments at least somewhat accountable to societal welfare constituencies. In post-soviet states, by contrast, the lack of democratic institutions often allowed either executive liberalizers or statist interests to dominate welfare policy-making.

It might be thought that my argument underestimates the significance of economic factors in explaining different welfare outcomes across Central Europe and the post-soviet states. It is true that the economic recessions were longer and more severe in the post-soviet states than in Central Europe, helping to account for deeper welfare cuts. But economic factors alone cannot explain many of the differences. During their recessions, for example, Poland and Hungary significantly increased some categories of welfare spending, while Russia and Kazakhstan cut spending. Patterns of liberalization across the cases do not correlate with economic or fiscal pressures; liberalizing policies were sometimes adopted during periods of fiscal stress but, in other cases, also during periods of strong economic recovery and growth. Moreover, all five states had substantially recovered their pre-1990 GDPs by 2000, and they continued to construct their welfare states very differently.[3] I argue that, while economic pressures forced cuts in welfare expenditures, politics influenced the shape of those cuts and the kinds of structural changes that were made in response.

The next sections of the paper provide evidence for the significance of political factors in explaining patterns of welfare state development and outcomes across the five cases. My central concern is how domestic politics mediated economic pressures for welfare state restructuring in Central European democracies and authoritarian and semi-authoritarian post-soviet states. Who influenced decisions to cut, preserve, or re-shape programs and entitlements across major areas of the inherited welfare states (health and education, social security and social assistance) and what are the consequences for welfare provision? I look at the efforts of societal and statist welfare constituencies to preserve old structures and benefits, and the efforts of liberalizing executives and technocratic modernizers to cut and re-shape them.

I focus first on the Russian Federation across three periods with distinct political and institutional configurations: the immediate post-transition period of executive hegemony; a period of incipient democratization in the mid-late 1990s; and a period of democratic decay and semi-authoritarianism from the end of the decade. The first period produced radical but largely failed liberalization efforts. During the second, the balance between liberalizing and anti-liberal state actors and legislative coalitions resulted in disabling deadlock over welfare state change. In the third, political shifts enabled successful liberalization even as economic conditions improved and fiscal pressures eased. Statist welfare interests re-asserted themselves to some extent in the latter periods, negotiating to preserve their roles and claims in a reformed system.

The analysis then considers more briefly the other four cases, which stand at opposite ends of the postcommunist spectrum in terms of democratic representation. Poland and Hungary are parliamentary democracies with more inclusive electoral and legislative institutions and less potential for concentration of executive power than Russia. Kazakhstan and Belarus became electoral-authoritarian or plebiscitary regimes early in the transition, with much more restrictive representative institutions and concentrated executive power than Russia.[4] In the communist period all five had broadly similar welfare state structures, providing low-level but comprehensive social security and services. All followed broadly similar postcommunist trajectories of transitional recession (though differing in length and depth), then economic recovery and resumed growth.[5]

Some scholars have proposed that electoral-authoritarian regimes may maintain inherited welfare structures despite the absence of democratic constraint, that plebiscitary democracy encourages 'presidential populism' and the continuation of old social contracts.[6] This study argues that societal interests have mattered little in authoritarian states. While elements of presidential populism are present in Belarus, they are not the major factor accounting for welfare state maintenance. Rather, I argue that it is primarily the political strength of statist interests that explains the maintenance of inherited welfare structures in Belarus, and the weakness of these interests that accounts for welfare state dismantling in Kazakhstan.

THE POST-SOVIET CASES

Three Stages of Welfare State Restructuring in Russia

How do these arguments about political interests and power explain welfare state outcomes in Russia? Political-institutional arrangements have shifted over the last decade. Russia had three distinct power constellations in which the strength of the executive and of representative institutions varied significantly. These shifts broadly explain patterns of welfare state change through the postcommunist period.

First Stage: Delegative Democracy and Non-Negotiated Welfare State Liberalization

In the first postcommunist period (1991-93), essentially one of 'delegative democracy,' concentrated executive power facilitated rapid welfare state change. Russia went through a period of virtually uncontested or 'non-negotiated' institutional restructuring. Policy power in the social sphere was assigned to insulated technocrats, who were placed in key positions within the government. Both societal and statist welfare interests were disorganized by the massive institutional shifts of the transition, and had little representation or influence. President Yeltsin largely ignored the protests of the legislature against his economic and social policy reforms, and in the end forcibly dissolved it.

During this period, liberal reformers and technocratic elites eliminated massive subsidy programs and fundamentally re-organized the welfare state. They decentralized the financing and administration of health and education, introduced privatization and insurance mechanisms, and off-loading social security obligations from the federal budget. As O'Donnell predicted in his analysis of delegative democracy, these unilateral policy changes proved to be of low quality. The institutional capacities needed to implement reforms were frequently absent. Local governments lacked the basic administrative structures and resources needed to run decentralized social services: competing providers were absent from most potential social markets and regulations for social insurance markets did not exist.[7] These changes contributed mainly to the decay of the state's welfare function, to large increases in poverty, inequality and exclusion from access to basic health and educational services. These radical reforms of the early 1990s illustrate the potential for rapid welfare state liberalization by a strong executive facing neither effective democratic constraints nor bureaucratic veto actors.

Second Stage: Liberalization Contested: the Politics of Polarization
With new legislative elections and the passage of the 1993 Constitution, from 1994 to 1999, the Russian polity underwent a process of incipient democratization that allowed some representation for pro-welfare interests.[8] Presidentialism and electoralism remained central and most formal democratic institutions shallow, but, as Michael McFaul characterizes the changes, "the core of a multiparty system emerged within the Russian parliament."[9] Political parties and the lower house of the *Duma* (legislature) took on a limited representative function and transformed the politics of welfare. Societal welfare state constituencies supported legislative parties—Women of Russia and Yabloko—that articulated and pursued a moderate reformist policy, seeking to preserve social protections and public sector spending. Health and especially education workers engaged in activism on a significant scale, becoming the most strike-prone sector of Russia's labor force, while trade unions built political alliances. Significant numbers of constituents were mobilized through new, semi-democratic political institutions. But moderate political parties remained extremely weak in Russia, and labor and other pro-welfare interests

were politically fragmented.[10] As a result, they managed to have only brief and limited influence on welfare policy.

In the mid-1990s, Russia's welfare politics gave way to a polarized politics, with unreformed, hard-left Communist successor parties dominating the legislature. For an extended period, the legislature blocked the executive's efforts at liberalization. The hard left, in tandem with state-bureaucratic welfare interests that had re-grouped, blocked further liberalization. The outcome of this period of 'politics of polarization' was an incoherent policy of retrenchment without restructuring, which led to the further decay and corruption of Russia's welfare state. In Russia's stratifying society, private spending on social services, both formal and informal, increased relative to public spending. The welfare state underwent a process of informalization, spontaneous privatization and parcelization of control over social security funds and social assets.

Third Stage: Managed Democracy and Liberalization
Negotiated Within the Elite
At the end of the 1990s, another major change in domestic political constellations created enabling conditions for welfare state liberalization in Russia. The December, 1999, Duma elections ended the left's dominance and the legislature's veto role, when a pro-executive legislative coalition became dominant. The deeper change in the political system to 'managed democracy' and presidential dominance, brought decay in the representative function of political parties.[11] As a consequence, political and societal constraints on welfare state change largely collapsed, allowing a breakthrough to liberalization. Between 2000 and 2003, the Duma approved changes in the legislative base across most areas of the welfare state, replacing the decayed welfare statist model. It reformed the pension system, introduced means-testing of social benefits, cut and regressed social taxes, and initiated new health and education reforms. Only the broadest and most visible benefit cuts were resisted by the legislature for fear of popular response. In sum, limits in representative institutions enabled a concentrated liberalization.

But Russia did not return to the 'non-negotiated liberalization' of the early 1990s. While democratic decay largely closed out representation of societal interests, state-based welfare elites retained some influence over welfare politics. Managed democracy produced its own distinctive mediation process of 'liberalization negotiated within the elite.' Social sector ministries were appeased by compensation strategies, mainly through the re-centralization of the welfare administration. The head of the Pension Fund warred with the Economic Development Ministry over privatization of pension funds.[12] Welfare policy-making focused around the competing interests of the liberalizing executive and statist welfare bureaucracies in controlling pools of social security funds and other social sector assets, with much less attention to the needs of the population.

The Russian case illustrates two patterns of non-democratic politics that are dysfunctional for welfare. In the first period, unconstrained executive domination led to rapid institutional change and state withdrawal from welfare provision. In the third period, limits on democratic representation allowed the executive and statist interests to dominate welfare policy, and while social sector ministries did make claims on expenditures, their primary interest was in protecting their institutional roles in welfare administration. The authoritarian polities of Kazakhstan and Belarus, respectively, illustrate these patterns more clearly.

Comparative Post-Soviet Cases

In Kazakhstan, President Nursultan Nazarbaev sharply cut social expenditures across most categories as the economy declined. During the early and mid-1990s, his administration dismantled the welfare programs inherited from the soviet period, as well as the ministerial structures that had administered them. The pension system was completely privatized by executive fiat.[13] A failed health insurance reform left an estimated one-quarter of the population without coverage, mainly in rural areas.[14] These policies were protested by the population, the political parties (those few that were allowed to operate in Kazakhstan's very constricted political space) and in the legislature, but these protests were met with repression and intimidation. Nazarbaev's power rested mainly in the security forces and in an oligarchic economic elite based in the private energy economy. Both the population and statist welfare bureaucracies lacked the capacity to defend welfare claims. By the end of the 1990s, Kazakhstan had the highest levels of private versus state medical expenditures, the lowest levels of social security coverage and by far the lowest levels of welfare state effort of the five cases considered here. In this case, unconstrained executive power substantially dismantled and privatized the welfare state, with minimal attention to either institutional context or social consequences.

In Belarus, by contrast, social programs and services were retained with little restructuring or privatization. Real expenditures were forced down by the recession, but welfare effort remained stable and in some areas increased slightly. The state continued to finance health care and education, and employment in these sectors grew during the 1990s. The social security system, though under severe financial stress, was kept in place.[15] Alyaksandar Lukashenka's regime, based largely in the old state-bureaucratic elite, maintained the old social contract.[16] But the continued dominance of statist interests in welfare policy meant the retention of old expenditure patterns, blocking changes that would have responded to transitional problems. Levels of poverty in Belarus remained high well into the economic recovery period despite substantial state welfare effort, indicating that expenditures were poorly allocated. Social security coverage remained high as did state expenditures for health care, but welfare provision remained bureaucratic and often inefficient, reflecting its prioritization of bureaucratic, rather than societal, interests.

THE CENTRAL EUROPEAN CASES

Welfare state reform also proceeded in Poland and Hungary during the 1990s. But the process of reform was for the most part more gradual and negotiated, involving more societal representation, contestation and compromise than in the post-soviet cases. In the East European context, stronger trade unions, more stable, moderate and socially oriented political parties, along with stronger governmental accountability gave welfare recipients a greater opportunity to participate in policy reform and for their interest to be represented in the policies. Welfare recipients were able to gain compensation for some welfare losses, and to retain a stronger state commitment to social provision. These trends were somewhat stronger in Poland than in Hungary, but both cases contrast sharply with post-soviet countries.

Both Poland and Hungary introduced major liberalizing structural reforms during the 1990s. Universal subsidies were eliminated, and most social assistance benefits were subject to means-testing. Both states partially privatized their pension systems. Private education and medical practices were legalized, and medical insurance introduced. But these changes were more modest and bargained than those in Russia or Kazakhstan, and more effective in limiting poverty and providing effective services than the stasis in Belarus. A predominant but not monopolistic state role in welfare provision provided better outcomes.

Though economic pressures were less prolonged and severe in these two cases, politics also played a major role in welfare outcomes. In both cases, electorates gave victories alternately to left and right-centrist parties through the 1990's. Reformed, essentially social-democratic parties played major governing roles, and they allied with national trade union federations. Negotiations that included political parties, trade unions and professional associations moderated the radical reform proposals that came from finance ministries. Though social-democratic parties did not always deliver on their electoral promises, they re-asserted the legitimacy of the state's welfare role against the neo-liberal orthodoxy.[17]

Societal influence is evident in bargaining over institutional changes such as pension reform. In both Poland and Hungary, initial reform proposals called for radical privatization. In the policy-making process, Labor and Social Ministries defended aspects of the old system, and government proposals were subject to public discussion as well as tripartite negotiations involving trade unions. In both cases reforms were substantially moderated through this process. In Poland, unions influenced financing provisions and gained concessions for their members. Meanwhile, in Hungary, the main social-democratic affiliated trade union gained concessions on generosity of benefits, state guarantees, and eligibility rules.[18] In both cases privatization would be phased in gradually, limiting effects on current recipients, preserving at least for a time a substantial state role in pension provision.

A similar process of negotiation and gradualism is evident in other reforms. In Poland, for example, initiatives to create a system of medical insurance began in the early 1990s. Political bargaining over the reform was long and contentious, with health sector unions, professional medical associations, political parties, and government bureaucracies all playing significant roles. In 1999, a compromise was finally reached that introduced an insurance mechanism while establishing strong state oversight and regulation.[19] The process took account of both the institutional context of the reform and the need to develop new regulatory institutions.

These examples illustrate the advantages of democratic bargaining in introducing institutional welfare state reforms. First, bargaining forces governments to take some account of societal interests and consequences. It moderates the extent and pace at which governmental actors can cut back on social commitments. Even in weak democracies, such as those in Central Europe, it gives some voice to organizations that can calculate the effects on social groups, and articulate their claims. By contrast, in the post-soviet states, institutional reforms were often passed with virtually no voice for those who would be affected. In the Russian pension reform, for example, societal representatives were invited into the process at a very late stage, when most of the legislation had already been prepared.[20] In Kazakhstan, the completed reform plan was made public only because the labor minister insisted.

The second effect is on the quality of reforms. Debate is likely to force consideration of the institutional and regulatory requirements, to avoid reforms that cannot be implemented because of massive institutional deficits. They provide both time and pressure for governments to build administrative capacity and the regulatory systems necessary to ensure the proper function of new social insurance markets and mechanisms. The more gradual liberalizing reforms in Central Europe generally proved to be more effective than the quick, condensed changes that were introduced by executives in the post-soviet region. The introduction of means-tested family benefits in Poland and Hungary, for example, restricted eligibility but did produce declines in poverty, especially among children, while similar reforms proved impossible to administer effectively in the post-soviet states.[21] When Central European governments did engage in rapid and largely non-negotiated reforms, as in the case of the 1992 health insurance reform in Hungary, the results tended to be poor and implementation ineffective.[22]

Democratic institutions in Central Europe also allowed societies some possibility to limit the broader social costs imposed by reforming governments. The 1993 election in Poland of the reformed post-Communist Democratic Left Alliance (DLA) constituted a rejection of shock-therapy reform, and brought to power a party that moderated (while still pursuing) liberalizing social reforms. The 1995 election of the Socialist Party in Hungary constituted a similar but largely unsuccessful protest. Under economic pressure, the Socialists adopted an austerity program that be-lied their election promises and the expectations of their trade union al-lies. Still, the Socialists maintained a commitment to welfare provision, and returned toward some of the electoral promises when economic pressures eased. The social-democratic parties that cycled in and out of government in the Central European states articulated a commitment to the state's welfare function against the neo-liberal orthodoxies that almost alone informed the welfare politics of executives in Russia and Kazakhstan.

The extent of democratic constraint in Poland and Hungary should not be exaggerated. During the 1990s, virtually all areas of their welfare states underwent retrenchment and privatization. The liberalizing ten-dency and its promoters were dominant. To some extent, the weakness of democratic constraint allowed governments to re-allocate spending to transitional problems, through eligibility restrictions on previously uni-versal benefits and increases in some expenditure categories at the ex-pense of others. Overall, though, Central European states produced bet-ter welfare maintenance and modernization. In comparison with Russia and Kazakhstan, Poland and Hungary have retained substantially higher proportions of public expenditures for social services, higher levels of social insurance coverage and secondary school attendance, and consid-erably higher levels of state welfare effort. And while they do not exceed Belarus on these measures, the Central European states have lower levels of poverty and more modern and efficient social services. These patterns emerged during the transition, and have been sustained through signifi-cant periods of economic recovery and growth.

CONCLUSION

What lessons can the Central European states offer post-soviet states about welfare state construction and provision? This study of three post-soviet states showed that their authoritarian and semi-authoritarian po-lities produced executive and bureaucratic dominance of welfare policy. In early postcommunist Russia and in Kazakhstan, largely unconstrai-ned executives introduced radical institutional reforms in health, edu-cation, and social security, reforms that disorganized existing systems of provision and failed in their own terms. They wasted both financial and administrative resources in welfare systems that were already under severe stress, and worsened service provision and inequalities of access.

These reforms illustrate the potential of unconstrained executives to produce rapid, low-quality policy change that takes little account of institutional context. Further, authoritarian leaders were able to make welfare state changes with little societal representation or accountability. Their policies were informed by an ideology of welfare state minimalism that could not be effectively contested in most periods. The consequences were large-scale, often informal privatization of social goods, state withdrawal and severe decay in the states' welfare functions. Economic stresses contributed much to these outcomes, but erratic, poorly-designed, non-negotiated policy changes exacerbated the effects of those stresses. Belarus shows a different pattern of bureaucratic domination that preserved the welfare state, but largely failed to adjust or modernize it. In all three cases, the weakness or absence of societal representation, the lack of societal voice or governmental accountability, produced policies that were poorly responsive to societal needs.

In the Central European cases, welfare state retrenchment and liberalization proceeded throughout the 1990s. But I have argued that their democratic systems provided some societal representation in bargaining over welfare state change. Bargaining produced more gradual, moderate and better-quality institutional reforms that were more effective in their own terms and in addressing social problems. Moreover, Central European societies had some opportunity to reject political leaders who imposed high social costs, and to elect parties that were committed to maintaining the state's welfare role even as they liberalized in response to financial constraints. The outcomes here were moderately liberalized welfare states, more effective institutional reforms that addressed poverty and other transitional problems, and sustained higher levels of welfare state effort.

The major lesson Central Europe offers for the post-soviet states is that democracy can bring welfare improvements. Most post-soviet states, including the three discussed here, have now gone through extended periods of economic recovery and growth. Economic and fiscal constraints on welfare state improvement have lessened. While real social expenditures have increased, the patterns of privatization and state withdrawal in Russia and Kazakhstan, and of stasis in Belarus, have largely been sustained through the recovery. Political changes that bring more representation for societal interests, and institutionalized pressures for governmental responsiveness, have the possibility to produce more and better welfare provision.

ENDNOTES

1. See Paul Pierson, *Dismantling the Welfare State: Reagan, Thatcher, ,and the Politics of Retrenchment* (Cambridge University Press, 1994); Robert R. Kaufman and Joan M. Nelson, eds, *Crucial Needs, Weak Incentives: Social Sector Reform, Democratization, and Globalization in Latin America* (Baltimore: Johns Hopkins University Press, 2004)

2. Guillermo O'Donnell, "Delegative Democracy," *Journal of Democracy,* January, 1994, vol. 5, no. 1, pp. 55-69; for applications of the concept, including in the post-socialist context, see: Guillermo O'Donnell, "On the State, Democratization, and Some Conceptual Problems: A Latin American View with Glances at Some Postcommunist Countries," *World Development* 21, (no. 8, 1993):. 1355-1369.

3. According to the World Bank, 2000 GDP as a percent of 1990 was 112 percent for Poland, 109 percent for Hungary, 90 percent for Kazakhstan, 88 percent for Belarus, and 64 percent for the Russian Federation; World Bank, *Transition: The First Ten Years: Analysis and Lessons for Eastern Europe and the Former Soviet Union* (Washington, D.C.: World Bank, 2002)

4. See Larry Diamond, "Thinking about Hybrid Regimes," in *Journal of Democracy* 13 (April 2002): 21-35, on regime classification. Diamond classifies Belarus as competitive authoritarian and Kazakhstan as hegemonic electoral authoritarian.

5. Data for the 1970s show that Hungary's welfare expenditure was higher, and Poland's slightly lower, than the Soviet average.

6. See, for example, Andrew March, "From Leninism to Karimovism: Hegemony, Ideology, and Authoritarian Legitimation," *Post-Soviet Affairs* 19 (October 2003): 307-336.

7. On delegative democracy and weak implementation of decisions in Russia see Eugene Huskey, *Presidential Power in Russia* (M.E. Sharpe, 1999), 161.

8. Major studies of the Russian polity that elaborate this process of 'incipient democratization,' though without necessarily using the term, include Michael McFaul, *Russia's Unfinished Revolution: Political Change from Gorbachev to Putin* (Cornell, 2001); Timothy J. Colton, *Transitional Citizens: Voters and What Influences Them in the New Russia* (Cambridge: Harvard Univ. Press, 2000); Timothy Colton and Jerry Hough, eds. *Growing Pains: Russian Democracy and the Election of 1993* (Washington, D.C.: Brookings Inst. 1998)

9. Michael McFaul, "Explaining Party Formation and Non-Formation in Russia: Actors, Institutions, and Choice," *Comparative Political Studies* 34 (December 2001): 1171.

10. See Walter Connor, *Tattered Banners: Labor, Conflict, and Corporatism in Postcommunist Russia* (Westview, 1996); Linda J. Cook, *Labor and Liberalization: Trade Unions in the New Russia* (Twentieth Century Fund, 1997)

11. Timothy J. Colton and Michael McFaul, *Popular Choice and Managed Democracy: The Russian Elections of 1999 and 2000,* (Washington, D.C.: Brookings, 2003)

12. See Linda J. Cook, "State Capacity and Pension Provision " in Timothy Colton and Stephen Holmes, eds., *The State After Communism: Governance in the New Russia,"* (Rowman and Littlefield, forthcoming, 2005).

13. See Mitchell A. Orenstein, *How Politics and Institutions Affect Pension Reform in Three Postcommunist Countries* (Policy Research Working Paper 2310) (Washington, D.C.: World Bank, March, 2000).

14. *Kazakhstan: Health Care Systems in Transition* (European Observatory on Health Care Systems, 1999). This reform was finally abandoned in 1998.

15. IMF, *Republic of Belarus: Selected Issues* (IMF Country Report No. 04/139. May, 2004), (Washington, D.C.: IMF, 2004), p. 8. Health and education increased from 14% to 18% of total employment between 1990 and 2002.

16. Steven M. Eke and Taras Kuzio, "Sultanism in Eastern Europe: The Socio-Political Roots of Authoritarian Populism in Belarus," *Europe-Asia Studies*, 52 (May 2000): 523-547.

17. Mitchell A. Orenstein, "The Return of the Left and its Impact on the Welfare State in Russia, Poland, and Hungary," in Linda J. Cook, Mitchell A. Orenstein, and Marilyn Rueschemeyer, eds., *Left Parties and Social Policy in Postcommunist Europe,* (Boulder: Westview Press, 1999), p. 83.

18. Orenstein, *How Politics and Institutions Affect Pension Reform*, p. 38.

19. Thomas Bossert and Cesary Wlodarczyk, "Unpredictable Politics: Policy Process of Health Reform in Poland," (Xerox, pre-Final Draft, January 4, 2000), quote is from p. 19.

20. Cook, "State Capacity and Pension Provision."

21. Michael F. Forster and Istvan Gyorgy Toth, "Child poverty and family transfers in the Czech Republic, Hungary, and Poland," *Journal of European Social Policy,* 11 (no. 4, 2001): 324-341.

22. Joan Nelson, "The Politics of Pension and Health-Care Reforms in Hungary and Poland," in Janos Kornai, Stephan Haggard, and Robert R. Kaufman, eds., *Reforming the State: Fiscal and Welfare Reform in Post-Socialist Countries,* (Cambridge: Cambridge University Press, 2001), . 235-266.

REFORMING IN-KIND PRIVILEGES AT THE REGIONAL LEVEL IN RUSSIA: POLITICAL DECISIONS AND THEIR DETERMINANTS

ANASTASSIA ALEXANDROVA,
POLINA KUZNETSOVA,
AND ELENA GRISHINA

INTRODUCTION

The modern Russian welfare system has evolved over several decades, and was initially created as a reflection of the redistributive policies of the socialist state. The first social privileges[1] were established in the 1930s, and between its inception and the mid–1980s they grew into a complex system of in-kind support for numerous categories of people, based on their status as 'deserving' or 'needy' individuals whom the state is obliged to honor or help.

When Russia began its transition to a market economy, it carried on the soviet system of privileges and, during the period of high inflation in the early 1990s, expanded the welfare state by adding new kinds of non-monetary assistance and broadening the categories of people who were eligible to receive benefits. Yet, the basic principles of social protection remained unchanged: privileges were granted on the basis of merits, professional hazards, vulnerability, but not on the basis of income. This growing mandate greatly exceeded the available government resources to finance all the privileges, so they became substantially underfinanced. The huge number of beneficiaries made the system cumbersome and difficult to manage, especially since people were able to receive duplicate privileges since the level of transparency was very low. Substantial budget resources were spent to finance privileges for the non-poor, and the amount of privileges received by the better-off and low-income people hardly differed, which increased vertical inequity.

As the Russian government began to realize that the system of privileges was economically unsustainable, failed to ensure financial transparency and was unsuccessful in targeting the poor, it introduced new national legislation in 2004 with a reform package that is now known both domestically and internationally as the 'monetization of privileges.' *Monetization* means cashing out of in-kind privileges, which is one of the necessary steps to increase efficiency and transparency of welfare expenditures. The new law transferred responsibility for welfare to the regional level, which meant that regional governments would become responsible for defining which beneficiaries would receive social privileges. Regional authorities could choose from a wide range of options: they could replace in-kind privileges to full or partial replacement with cash benefits (monetization) or to leave the welfare system untouched, but assume full responsibility for their financing and provision. This chapter aims to measure the degree and distribution of monetization at the regional level in Russia and use this data to explain factors that affected policy decisions on monetization. We hope to determine, in the final analysis, the level to which the reform objectives have been attained.

Section one briefly describes the key features of the system of privileges in the Russian Federation, emphasizing the need for transformation and the content of the monetization reforms. Section two presents the data sources and methodology used to measure and analyze monetization in this study. Specifically, in this section we present the index of monetization constructed for this purpose. Section three illustrates the scale of regional monetization, allowing comparisons between regions on the basis of the index. Estimates of the regression model used to reveal the factors that are associated with regional policy decisions on monetization are introduced and interpreted in the section four.

The study led us to conclude that social policy making at the regional level is not entirely an *ad hoc* process: resource constraints, political economy and socio-demographic factors are significant determinants of regional responses to the rules established by federal legislation. Monetization at the regional level appears to be a product of rational planning by the executive authorities (considering resource constraints against potential liabilities) and political consensus. One lesson that can be gleaned from this study is that the federal government ought to pay attention to the factors that affect regional policy making, in order to predict the success or failure of future national reforms. The study also suggests that wealthier regions, especially those led by more recently elected governors, are best at implementing national initiatives and should be considered for pilot projects.

REFORM OF IN-KIND PRIVILEGES IN RUSSIA

The features of Russia's social protection system have been widely documented[2]. Inherited from the Soviet society that was 'a status society,'[3] it provided support to four broad categories:

- traditionally considered vulnerable, such as the disabled and pensioners,
- merit groups (e.g., labor heroes, WW II veterans, Communist Party *nomenklatura*)
- occupational categories, such as military servants, judges etc., and
- victims of natural or human and professional hazards, (e.g., the Chernobyl catastrophe)

Throughout the Soviet period, the number of beneficiary categories within each broad group grew: as the state become richer, new benefits were gradually introduced. But although benefits changed, the principles behind providing in-kind benefits remained the same. These principles dictated that, since all resources and assets were controlled by the state, the state would reinforce its control by making the choice of services to be provided to individuals, rather than delegating the choice to consumers (beneficiaries). Moreover, the protection of the poor was not among policy priorities in the Soviet Union, since the phenomenon of poverty was not officially recognized. As a result, the fact that many of the beneficiaries of social privileges were among the better-off, was not considered inappropriate. The principle was: "assistance to "the weak" combined with favors for "the strong""[4].

When the transition to a market economy began in the early 1990s and new phenomena—such as wage arrears and poverty—were no longer taboo, Russia not only maintained its soviet-era welfare policy, but continued to expand its already broad and complex system of privileges and compensations. In part, this response was intended to counter the economic shocks of the transition: the government believed that granting more in-kind privileges would balance the effects of inflation. By the mid-1990s, there were more than 150 types of privileges, covering over 230 categories of the population[5]. This large set of nationally mandated benefits was complemented by numerous regional and local initiatives, which introduced additional privileges or expanded existing ones to other apply to individuals in other social categories. For instance, in Perm oblast, additional benefits (free commuter transportation) were introduced for pensioners who had worked longer than 35 years in the Far North. Another additional group of beneficiaries defined by Perm regional legislation comprises schoolchildren living in large families, where the total number of children exceeds 3. These are just two examples of many hundreds or perhaps thousands of variations, which have never been studied in detail or summarized.

There were several problems with this system of in-kind privileges. First, the system could not be adjusted easily to reach the most needy groups. For instance, the provision of low-cost or free energy benefits those who possesses more electric appliances and light sources (thereby consuming more electricity) the most. Better-off households benefit more from housing privileges in the same way. Transportation benefits are regressive in a different manner, since by default they exclude the people who are not able to use transportation because they either live in rural areas not served by public transport, or have physical constraints that do not permit them to travel.

The second problem was that decisions to introduce new privileges were taken at the federal level, but regional or local budgets were responsible to fund these mandates. The poorest areas, therefore, were the least able to cover the high cost of the public welfare program. While service providers, such as landlords, transportation companies and clinics, nevertheless honored welfare guidelines, which translated into lost revenues for these providers, creating an additional burden for regional and local economies and preventing effective enterprise restructuring.

Third, the lack of transparency in resource allocation further burdened the welfare system. Given the design of the system and Russia's extremely weak administrative capacity, the consumption of many privileges could not be made transparent, which meant that fraud was rampant. For example, since there was no mechanism for tracing how many pensioners (who were permitted to ride for free) used public transportation, how many times a day and for what distance, transportation companies made arbitrary estimates of these figures. The fiscal authority, in turn, which had no means of verifying these estimates, reacted with an equally arbitrary response: allotting the transportation companies state resources depending on what was available.

In short, the driving force for welfare reform has been to counter the problems posed by the system of privileges, which is economically unsustainable, non-transparent and fails to target the poor. The transformation of in-kind privileges to cash benefits, or monetization, was meant to increase the transparency of the expenditures, to give beneficiaries freedom to choose which benefits served them best and to simplify the administration. In order to achieve the goal of creating an affordable system, the targeting of benefits to low-income groups and the reduction of beneficiary categories must complement monetization. Not all of these steps were followed, as will be described below.

The August 22, 2004 "The Law on Monetization" divided the large set of financial responsibilities between the federal government and the regions. The new system of privileges for several large categories (veterans of labor, victims of political repression, home front workers during World War II) was re-defined as the "system of social protection measures" and was to be financed entirely by the regions. At the same time, there were other categories of welfare recipients (for example, people with disabilities or veterans of World War II), for whom the social protection measures became the responsibility of the federal government. For these 'federal groups,' the law specified details, such as the amount of monthly cash payments, which replaced some of the removed privileges and the remaining set of in-kind assistance to which they are entitled. The table in Annex 1 illustrates this split into federal and regional groups with some detail.

The design of the Law on Monetization is rather contradictory. On the one hand, it gives the regions full freedom to decide how they can make their social protection resources more transparent, better targeted to the poor and more efficient. The regions are not required to maintain the same privileges for all the categories that had existed in the previous system. Theoretically, they can introduce targeting within the existing categories that fall under their domain. On the other hand, the federal government is not similarly required to reform its welfare practices, since eligibility for federal groups remains untouched, the federal government's reforms do not target the poor and only a handful of privileges were removed (mostly those providing benefits to public sector employees, such as free city transportation for the police or fire brigades employees). Moreover, the delineation between "federal" and "regional" groups of recipients is non-transparent and not clear to the population or even the authorities. As the regions were given responsibility for larger groups (veterans of labor are the largest group of privilege recipients) they have had more difficulty to match their obligations with adequate resources. Yet, they must also adhere to the clause, which requires that the situation of people who are still eligible to receive benefits be maintained by the new welfare system. Thus, the regions received mixed political signals from the federal level and have a strong disincentive for introducing targeting measures or cashing out most of the in-kind privileges. In the next section, we offer an overview of how different regions reacted to these mixed signals and what may have been possible determinants of the observed variations in monetization.

DATA SOURCES AND METHODOLOGY

For the analysis presented in this chapter, we used two data sets on monetization of in-kind privileges. The first dates back to November-December 2004, when the Institute for Urban Economics conducted a formal survey of the regional authorities, asking them to outline all of the details of regional laws and to determine social protection measures for veterans of labor and other 'regional privileged groups,' as defined by the federal Law on Monetization. The second data set is derived from a database of regional legislation adopted in March-April 2005. The first data set contains 58 cases because of attrition. The second set (regional legislation) covers 79 regions, for which the legislation databases are completed.

The first issue we had to address was how to compare regional actions concerning monetization. Let us suppose that Region A monetizes only 1 benefit (free transportation) and Region B wants to monetize three benefits (dental services, electricity and solid fuel provision). Which benefits are more important and which need to be monetized first? From the economic perspective, the free provision of housing, utilities and transportation are the costliest benefits and cannot be easily rationalized by market failures, unlike, for instance, health benefits. But how do we measure their relative importance against each other and against other privileges? Do the three monetized benefits of the Region B represent three times more important decision than monetization of transportation benefit by Region A? Part of the problem is that we were unable to use the number of privilege users, since, as described in Section 1, for many privileges the number of actual beneficiaries and the intensity of use are unknown. Fiscal data on spending by type of privilege has not been generated either. A related problem is how to compare monetization of privileges provided previously to different groups of the population. In other words, if Region A is cashing out transportation to the labor veterans and Region B does the same for home front workers, which of them is making a more important step towards efficiency of social protection? These questions motivated our study and made us suggest a measure that is based on the actual observations of regional decisions rather than on subjective judgments.

Index of monetization

To construct the measure of monetization taking place at the regional level, we narrowed the focus of the study, to consider the three largest groups of 'regional beneficiaries,' i.e., labor veterans, home front veterans and former political prisoners. Annex 1 gives an overview of in-kind privileges that these groups had been receiving before the reforms took place. Since these privileges are quite numerous, we included a sub-set of them in the analysis, focusing on free or discounted provision of the most widely used services, leaving aside such privileges as no-interest credit for housing construction or coverage of funeral costs. Table 1 below lists the groups and privileges that have been included in this analysis.

Table 1: Benefit user groups and privileges they received prior to 2005.

Benefit user groups	Labor veterans	Home front veterans	Former political prisoners
Types of benefits	Denture services	Denture services	Denture services
	Urban, suburban and intercity transportation	Urban, suburban and intercity transportation	Urban and suburban transportation
	Railroad and water commuter services.	Railroad and water commuter services	Railroad transportation
	–	50% discount on provision of medicines	50% discount on provision of medicines
	Housing and utility	–	Housing and utility
	Telephone services	–	Telephone connection services
	Solid fuel provision	–	Solid fuel provision
	Wired-radio services	–	–
	Antenna services	–	–
	–	–	Sanatorium-resort therapy

Looking at the Table 1, one can see that of the privileges included in this analysis, a given region can monetize all 20 listed in the table, or some fraction thereof. In order to compare the relative importance of these benefits, we determined which privileges for which groups were the least or most frequently monetized across the regions, first according to the December survey and then to the adopted regional legislation. The most unique decisions interested us most, as we assumed that they were the most difficult to implement. The outcomes corresponded to our initial hypothesis of which would be the most important privileges to be monetized: housing and transportation. Indeed, of the five regions that had intended to monetize housing benefits in December, only four actually followed through. City transportation was the second least frequently monetized of the privileges. Small privileges, such antenna or radio services are on the opposite side—they were monetized almost universally.

Based on these observations, we issued weights to each of the 20 privileges, which are inversely proportional to the frequency of their monetization. In other words, the more regions monetize a given benefit, the less weight it gains in construction of the overall index. The weights obtained from April data (for easier comparison of two data sets) are given in Table 2, with the most highly weighted indicated by italics.

Table 2: Weights of benefits used in the monetization index

	April
Labor veterans	
Denture services	0.03[6]
Municipal, suburban and intercity passenger transportation services	*0.06*
Railroad and water commuter services.	0.02
Housing and utility services	*0.22*
Telephone services	0.02
Wired–radio services	0.02
Community antenna services	0.02
Dry fuel services	*0.08*
Home front veterans	
Denture services	0.03
Municipal, suburban and intercity passenger transportation services	*0.06*
Railroad and water commuter services	0.02
Provision of medicines	0.03
Former political prisoners	
Sanatorium–resort therapy	0.02
Provision of medicines	0.03
Denture services	0.03
Railroad transportation services	0.02
Municipal and suburban transportation services	0.02
Housing and utility services	*0.18*
Telephone connection services	0.03
Solid fuel	*0.08*

The methodology of constructing the index measure of monetization is provided in Annex 2. In short, for each region we created a set of 20 dummies corresponding to 20 privileges; each dummy takes a value of 1 if a given privilege is monetized, and 0 if it was not. The weights are used to multiply each dummy value accordingly, and the sum of these weighted dummies is the index value for each region. In other words, the index is higher when more benefits are cashed out. It is particularly high for the regions that had the courage to monetize housing and transportation benefits. The minimum possible index value is 0 (not a single privilege is monetized) and the maximum is 100 (full monetization). The distribution of the regions by index values is presented in Annex 3 and will be discussed in Section 3.

THE MODEL

We used the proposed index not only to compare the degree of monetization across Russian regions, but also in an attempt to find out possible determinants of the observed variations. Using the index as a dependent variable, we estimate a simple regression model that considers the regional response to the national Law On Monetization as a function of the two parameters:

- *Affordability.* We assume that rational regional authorities will be more interested in introducing monetization when it is affordable. Affordability is influenced both by regional resources and potential liabilities; the latter, in turn, depends on how many people belonging to the three considered groups of beneficiaries live in a region. Our hypothesis is that the greater the resources, the higher the degree of monetization, and the greater the number of beneficiaries, the lower the incentive to monetize.

- *Political acceptance.* We also assume that the more beneficiaries there are, the more likely they will be to generate protests against monetization. Similarly, we believe that population density would have a negative effect on the degree of monetization, because regions with high population density would have a greater risk of social mobilization against reforms and protests in such regions would be more sizeable. Political parameters of the region (electoral activity, proportions of left-wing or right-wing voters) are assumed to be significant determinants of the acceptance of monetization as perceived by policy makers. Heavy political weight of a governor in the region may be an important positive correlate of monetization as it is associated with more 'obedient' regional parliaments.

These parameters are difficult to assess directly and we clarify our hypotheses by use of several proxies:

– To approximate regional resources we use variables that characterize regions as richer or more attractive to the population. These are: per capita gross regional product; per capita investments; per capita budget spending on social protection. In addition, we introduce a dummy to separate the regions that were donors in 2004 as defined in the inter-budgetary system by the Russian Ministry of Finance. Not directly related to regional resources is the variable characterizing migration growth rate in the region. Since, according to the Russian statistics[7], higher migration growth rates are observed in more attractive, richer regions we assume that it would be positively associated with monetization.

– To approximate potential liability, we include the percentage of households receiving privileges in the region, expecting it to have a positive effect on monetization because a large number of privilege users creates heavier burdens for the economy, and rational authorities would try to reduce it through monetization.

– As proxies to political acceptance, we introduce voting parameters. The risk of protest actions is assumed to be higher (and monetization, therefore, lower) in the regions with a high proportion of the Communist Party and other left-wing voters. Alternatively, a lower risk of protests and a higher monetization are expected in regions with a high proportion of Unified Russia voters. Additionally, high voter turnout during the last Duma elections (which is highly correlated with the level of voting for the Unified Russia—the value of correlation coefficient equals 0.84) most likely implies the use of the so-called 'administrative resource,' i.e., the ability of governing authorities to mobilize voters to demonstrate support for the Kremlin's policies. In this situation, we would expect the current

Governor to have a great influence in the region and therefore able to introduce monetization easily, without the threat of protests.

– An important variable in this group is the share of the rural population in a region. Rural residents gain more from privilege monetization because many in-kind benefits had been inaccessible to them. A high proportion of rural population should increase the incentive to monetize, affecting the index positively.

– Human factors, such as the characteristics of regional Governors and their political importance are difficult to measure. We use the length of incumbency of the current governor as a proxy of his/her stability and support, and expected it to have a negative effect on monetization, since experienced political survivors would likely be more cautious. We also supposed that if a Governor faces forthcoming reelections, he/she would be less willing to deal with monetization and hence we look at the number of months left before the next election. We also assume that if the governor has been enjoying support from the population, he/she would go for monetization with a lesser degree of caution, and we include a variable reflecting percentage of voters who supported the current governor at the last elections, expecting it to affect monetization positively. We also expected that federal policy, specifically the decision to abolish elections of the governors and make them assigned by the president, would reduce the importance of voter-related factors to regional decision-makers.

– Finally, to control for unobservable parameters that may vary across groups of regions and may also be associated with the role that the president's Plenipotentiary Representatives play in the federal districts that they supervise, we introduce six dummy variables corresponding to six of the seven federal districts[8] that encompass all of Russia.

To make sure that the model is linear (this was important, since the dependent variable is a constructed one), we ran a Ramsey nonlinearity test, which then enables us to estimate this model using backward stepwise regression. The final model estimates contain significant variables only and are presented in Section 4.

SCALE AND DISTRIBUTION OF MONETIZATION

The index of monetization permits a comparison of how many regions intended to introduce greater or lesser degrees of monetization (58 cases based, on the December survey data) and how many of them fulfilled their intentions (79 cases). First, we observed that the degree of monetization overall can be at best called 'modest,' since the median index values were 28 in December and in 33 April.

The left part of Chart 1 shows that quite many regions had no intention to introduce monetization in December (far left peak) and another large group went half-way ahead (center peaks)—transforming some privileges and keeping others in-kind. The right tail of the distribution represents the regions that had the highest monetization index values in December. Annex 3 gives index values for each region, showing, for instance, that in December the highest monetization proposals were made in Tver region, Republic of Tatarstan, Vologda region, Leningrad region and Tumen region.

The right part of Chart 1 demonstrates a similar distribution of regions by index value based on April data. The left tail grew somewhat, while the right one became smaller and the highest concentration is observed in the middle. This is a visual demonstration of the fact that monetization occurred at the very moderate level and that the most preferred way for the Russian regions was partial monetization[9].

Chart 1: Distribution of regions by index values.

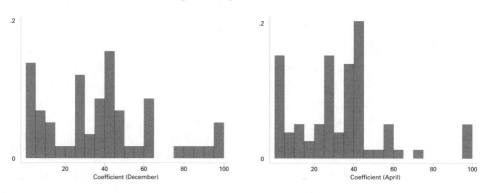

In absolute numbers, the review of regional legislation on the 20 privileges in question gives the picture presented in Table 3.

Table 3: Number of regions by type of their response to monetization (N=79).

	Labor veterans	Home front workers	Victims of political repressions
In-kind privileges remain	10	17	9
Partial monetization	65	34	67
Full	4	28	3

We see that there are only three regions (Tver, Tatarstan and Yamalo-Nenetsky autonomous area—see Annex 3 for details) that fully mone-tized privileges across the categories. Their index values reach the maxi-mum of 100. The majority, as Chart 1 also shows, monetized part of the privileges. Breaking it down by beneficiary groups shows that regions were more courageous to monetize privileges for home front workers (who are not a numerous group and who had the smallest number of privileges provided to them, as shown in Section 2). About one-fifth left the system of privileges untouched.

With two sets of data available, we could try to link changes in the index value observed between April and December with the intensity of subsequent protests. We do not mean to imply that there is a causal rela-tionship between the protests and the final legislative outcome. On the contrary, there may be many other reasons to explain the differences in intent and the final legislation. Policy making at the regional level is a parliamentary process, originating in the executive branch (line minis-tries draft legislation and analyze the expected impact) and continuing in regional parliaments, which make final decisions about the content of legislation. In December data, we assume that the executive branch made suggestions on what ought to be monetized, based on a cost-benefit analy-sis and taking into account resource constraints and future liabilities to the population. The April dataset is derived from the legislation that was the product of parliamentary discussions during which other factors, such as the balance of political power, may have played a more important role. These parliamentary discussions took place mostly during the period of active protests, but we do not know to what extent the discussion results were affected by the protests.

Chart 2 shows that between December and April, some regions that intended to monetize privileges fully ended up with a more modest degree of monetization, while those who had declared no monetization in December eventually introduced limited reforms by April. The vertical axis reflects the degree of change. If a dot is placed above the central 'zero' line, it means that a given region introduced more monetization in April than had been planned in December. Below the 'zero' line are the regions that withdrew from the plans declared in the December survey. The horizontal axis presents monetization index values constructed for December, i.e., the closer a dot is to the right, the higher the index value for a corresponding region in December. In other words, we see that a group of regions that intended to monetize more (right side of the chart) mostly falls below the 'zero' line, meaning that these intentions were not realized. On the left side, we see many regions with an initially low index, but which moved above the zero line—meaning that more monetization was introduced in April than had been planned in December.

Chart 2: Changes of index values between December and April.

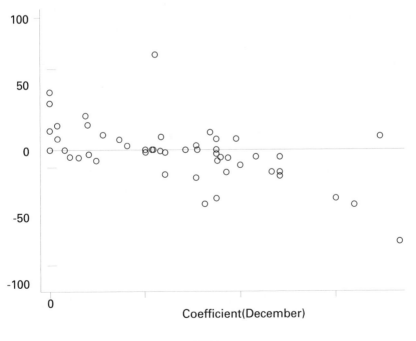

The regions that withdrew from their intentions included the Vologda region (which had intended to cash out housing privileges but ended up keeping them as in-kind privileges while reducing the amount of the monthly cash benefit from 700 to 500 rubles), Leningrad and Kostroma regions and the Republic of Buryatia. Virtually no changes were made by nine of the regions: among them were those with high monetization (Tatarstan and Tver), partial monetization (Lipetsk, Kaluga and Penza regions) and the complete absence of monetization (Novgorod). Finally, the Yamalo-Nenetski autonomous area, Volgograd and Voronezh regions made up the most interesting group. These regions intended to keep most or all privileges in kind, but ultimately cashed out many or (in the case of Yamalo-Nenetski area) all of them.

The main message of Chart 2 is that it is hard to claim that protests, all of which occurred between the two points of observation, universally reduced the scale of monetization. When we looked specifically at the regions where protests were massive (more than 10,000 participants according to the Russian Political Culture Research Center—protest movement was especially intensive in 20 regions, among them Tatarstan, Bashkiria, Udmurtia, Saint-Petersburg, Moscow region, Belgorod region, Voronezh region, Primorje territory), we realized that these regions can be found in all parts of Chart 2 i.e., among those that reduced the degree of monetization, among those that maintained monetization levels (in most cases) and even among those that introduced more reform than had been initially planned. Very revealing is the fact that the most active protests occurred in regions that did not intend to implement full monetization, which means that one cannot conclude that the protests were against monetization specifically, rather than against reforms in general. The overall effect of the changes introduced between December and April during the parliamentary discussions of drafted legislation appears to be 'center-focused,' i.e., most of the regions ended up with a moderate degree of monetization.

REGRESSION MODEL ESTIMATES

Table 4 shows the model estimates based on the April data. One can immediately see that many of the hypotheses presented earlier were not proved by the data, as many of the suggested variables turned out to be insignificant. The resulting set of factors, however, yields several interesting observations.

Table 4: Findings of the regression analysis (monetization index used as dependent variable)

Monetization index, April	
Const	−41.48** (−2.45)
Donor region	16.42*** (2.81)
Social protection expenditures	5.89*** (2.71)
Net migration	0.10** (2.12)
Density of the population	−0.02** (−2.36)
Proportion of privilege recipients in the population	0.56*** (2.80)
Voter turnout	1.06*** (3.87)
Experience of the Governor	−1.21** (−2.24)
Central Federal District dummy	9.70* (1.80)
N	79
F-statistics	6.27
R^2-adj	0.35

Note. t-values are in parentheses; *** corresponds to 1%, ** – to 5%, and * – to 10% significance.

First, we see that both economic and political factors can be found among the factors that influenced the monetization scale. Richer regions introduced a greater degree of monetization, as is demonstrated by the first three variables in the table. Perhaps this effect is due to the fact that wealthier regions were better able to introduce higher cash payments to make their electorates and beneficiaries happier. Any conclusion about direct relationship between monetization scale in a region and its status of a rich and attractive community is difficult to establish *a priori*, since different factors play a role here: on the one hand, it is easier for a rich region to start a large-scale reform but, on the other hand, due to its greater autonomy from the center, it may resist the federal government's pressure to monetize more actively. According to our model estimates, the factor of resources is stronger than government pressure.

The high proportion of welfare recipients among the population has a small but significant effect, proving the hypothesis that the authorities were trying to be rational about the burden that in-kind privileges create for their economies, especially when federal funding of these privileges for the 'regional categories' was withdrawn. Administrative costs may be another explanation behind this. It will be easier for the budget to pay cash benefits to a larger number of people, than to finance the continued provision of housing, transportation and other services that many people may never use.

It was quite surprising that the rural population did not have much of an effect on the outcome of welfare reforms. It may be that regional authorities saw no use in giving much weight to the interests of rural residents, who tend to be less politically active and, in most regions, represent a minority of the population.

The voter turnout might at least indicate the degree to which citizens tend to be law-abiding (or, more specifically, a low voter turnout may indicate general public apathy and disappointment with the regional government and elections in general). Bearing in mind that the voter turnout is evidently correlated with the proportion of Unified Russia votes, it is possible to suggest that voter turnout simply reflects the so-called 'administrative resources' of the government, meaning that the population is perceived to be under the government control. Regions with higher voter turnout probably have greater public confidence in government, and thus may expect greater public support for reforms. This is how we interpret the positive influence of voter turnout on the index of monetization.

The high degree of support for the governor at elections did not have the expected positive impact on monetization, which we attribute to external forces: at the end of 2004, regional governor elections were abolished and governors have since been appointed by the president. Yet, the salience of the length of a regional governor's incumbency was confirmed. The length of incumbency affects monetization negatively, since experienced governors are presumably more cautious and have the experience and power to bargain with the federal center in order to postpone or avoid implementation of unpopular reforms.

CONCLUSIONS

One of the important observations derived from this analysis is that the system of in-kind privileges has not really been reformed at the regional level. The original categories of beneficiaries remain universally used and the degree of monetization, as measured by the suggested index, has been modest. Russian regions responded to the contradictory federal legislation with a great degree of caution and have largely lost an opportunity to substantially reform their social protection systems. The majority of the regions retained in-kind privileges, such as free provision of solid fuels, dental prosthetic services and even spa treatments (to victims of political repression).

Nevertheless, some very positive initiatives can be seen as well. First, there are at least two regions that reformed housing privileges despite the fact that federal legislation did not affect them. Canceling such privileges and introducing cash benefits is rational, from the perspective of the regional governments, because a program of housing subsidies for the poor has been operating in Russia for several years and will be able to protect people who may not benefit from monetization.

The model's findings suggest that social policy making at the regional level is not entirely an *ad hoc* process that cannot be quantitatively analyzed. On the contrary, by using a monetization index constructed through observations of monetization decisions, we were able to show that resource constraints, political context and socio-demographic factors are significant determinants of regional responses to the rules established by federal legislation. Monetization at the regional level appears to be a product of rational planning by the executive authorities (considering resource constraints against potential liabilities) and political consensus.

One policy lesson from the analysis is quite obvious: the federal government ought to pay attention to the factors that affect regional policy making, since knowledge of these factors may help to predict the success or failure of future national reforms. It would be even more important to conduct political discussions between federal and regional authorities, based on an analysis of the possible implications of reform. The study also suggests that while reforming social protection programs proved to be challenging everywhere in Russia, wealthier regions, especially those led by more recently elected governors, are best at implementing national initiatives. These regions should be considered for pilot projects, since they are more willing to introduce reforms aimed at improving the transparency and efficiency of social expenditures. On the other hand, regions led by conservative long-term governors or those with fewer resources to support reforms are likely to require special treatment, ranging from closer consultation, monitoring or guidance, to temporary financial aid that could relieve short-term negative effects and encourage more radical transformation.

ENDNOTES

1. By 'privileges' or *l'goty* in Russian we imply goods and services, such as transportation, housing, energy, medicines, provided by the state for free or at substantially reduced prices.

2. Anastassia Alexandrova, Lilia Ovcharova and Sergey Shishkin, *Bednost' i l'goty: mify i realnost'* (Moscow: Boell Foundation, 2003), 25-38; Rostislav Kapelushnikov, "Russia's Social Safety Net: Standing at the Cross-Roads," In Reiner Weichhardt, ed., *Economic developments and reforms in cooperation partner countries: the role of the state with particular focus on security and defense issues* (Ljubljana: NATO, 1998), 189-193.

3. Kapelushnikov, "Russia's Social Safety Net," 191.

4. Kapelushnikov, "Russia's Social Safety Net," 191.

5. Alexandrova, Ovcharova and Shishkin, *"Bednost' i l'goty,"* 29.

The Table contains truncated values of weights so their sum may not equal to 1.

Statistical handbook: *Social'noe polozhenie i uroven' zhizni naseleniya Rossii* (Moscow: Goskomstat of Russia, 2004).

Omitted variable is for the North-Western district.

In the final picture, minimum index values are observed in Chukotsky autonomous area, Republic of North Ossetia and Khabarovsk territory. Leaders of monetization are Tver region, the Republic of Tatarstan and Yamalo-Nenetsky autonomous area.

Annex 1: Federal and regional beneficiaries as defined by Law on Monetization (selected illustrations)

Beneficiaries	Benefits before 'monetization'	In-kind benefits remaining in 2005	Cash benefits introduced since 2005
RESPONSIBILITY OF THE FEDERAL BUDGET STARTING FROM 2005			
World War 2 veterans and participants (total 8 sub-categories within this group)	1. 50% discount on housing and utility services 2. 50% discount on guard services for single living persons or pairs 3. Free provision of medicines 4. Free denture services 5. Free provision of prosthetic devices 6. Free urban, suburban and intercity transportation 7. Railroad and water commuter services. 8. One time in two years (or 50% discount for one time a years) free two–way ticket on railroad, water, air, bus services.	1. 50% discount on housing and utility services 2. Free provision of prosthetic devices	2000 Rubles (to WW2 invalids), 1500 Rubles (WW2 participants), 1100 or 600 Rubles (others) (come into force from 1 January 2006)
Disabled	1. Free provision and repair of technical means of rehabilitation or compensation for bought technical means. 2. Free provision of transportation means or compensation for transportation services. 3. Free provision of medical and domestic services (if needed) 4. 50% discount on telephone and wired-radio services 5. For not working — free provision of sanatorium–resort therapy 6. For working — privileged provision of sanatorium–resort therapy 7. For disabled and their attendants — Urban, suburban and intercity transportation 8. For disabled or for a disabled person (1 degree) and his attendant —50% discount on railroad water, air commuter services in period 1 Oct. till 15 May or one time a year free two–way ticket on railroad, water, air, bus services in other period. 9. For disabled person (I and II degree) and for disabled child — one time a year free two–way ticket to the place of treatment.	1. Free provision and repair of technical means of rehabilitation or compensation for bought technical means. 2. Free parking on special cars	1. 1400, 1000, 800 or 500 Rubles, depending on the degree of disability, as defined by the state expertise (come into force from 1 January 2006) 2. Payment for transportation to prosthetic-orthopedic organization (depending on transportation cost) 3. Payment for accommodation when they are traveling to prosthetic-orthopedic organization (depending on number of days lived)
Blood donors	1. Free meals in a day of blood taking 2. Day of blood taking and next day are not working day with usual wage pay 3. The wage rises twice if the day of blood taking is holiday 4. In special cases (depending on amount of blood taken) the scholarship rises by 25% for 6 months 5. In special cases (depending on amount of blood taken) the allowance on temporary disability is equal to the wage 6. for honorary donors — denture services 7. for honorary donors — 50% discount on medicines 8. for honorary donors — Urban, suburban transportation 9. for honorary donors — 50% discount on communal services 10. for honorary donors — confessional loan for accommodation building	1. Free meals on a day of blood taking	1. In special cases (depending on amount of blood taken) the allowance on temporary disability is equal to the wage 2. for honorary donors — 6000 Rub. a year

Annex 1: continued

Beneficiaries	Benefits before 'monetization'	In-kind benefits remaining in 2005	Cash benefits introduced since 2005
RESPONSIBILITY OF THE FEDERAL BUDGET STARTING FROM 2005			
Chernobyl	1. The size of old-age pension is increased by 30% for Chernobyl liquidators (3 category), 25% for Chernobyl liquidators (4 category). 2. In case of death — pension for loss of breadwinner is paid to dependants. 3. In case of death —monthly compensation to each dependant: 50% of minimal size of old-age pension 4. In case of death — yearly compensation to children: MMW 5. *The age of retirement is decreased depending on category.(?)* 6. Yearly payments for 1 and 2 category of people: 5*MMW or 4*MMW, depending on disability group 7. Yearly payments — for 3 category: 3*MMW, for 4 category: 2*MMW or MMW 8. One –time compensation for 2 category of people: 100* MMW, 70* MMW or 50* MMW, depending on disability group 9. 50% discount on housing and utility services 10. 50% discount on solid fuel provision 11. For 1,2,3 category of people — free provision of medicines (for 4 category —50% discount) 12. For 1,2,3 category of people — denture services (for 4 category —50% discount) 13. For 1 and 2 category of people — urban, suburban and intercity transportation 14. For 1,2,3 category of people — one time a year free trip to the place of treatment 15. For 1 and 2 category of people — one time a year free trip to the place of treatment 16. For 1, 2,3 category of people — accommodation if needed 17. For 3 category of people —50% discount for two-way ticket on railroad, water, air, bus services. 18. Monthly payments: 5000 Rub., 2500 Rub., 1000 Rub., depending on the degree of disability 19. Increase in scholarship by 50% 20. Compensation for food products — 300 /200 Rub., depending on category	1. 50% discount on housing and utility services 2. 50% discount on solid fuel provision	1. The size of old-age pension is increased by 30% for Chernobyl liquidators (3 category), 25% for Chernobyl liquidators (4 category). 2. In case of death — pension for loss of breadwinner is paid to dependants. 3. In case of death — 10000 Rub. for families, 5000 Rub. for parents. 4. In case of death —monthly compensation to each dependant: 92,66 Rub. 5. In case of death — yearly compensation to children: 100 Rub. 6. Yearly payments for 1 and 2 category of people: 500 Rub. or 400 Rub., depending on disability group 7. Yearly payments — for 3 category: 300 Rub., for 4 category: 200 or 100 Rub.. 8. One –time compensation for 2 category of people: 10000, 7000 or 5000 Rubles, depending on disability group 9. Monthly payments: 5000 Rub., 2500 Rub., 1000 Rub., depending on the degree of disability 10. Monthly compensations: 250 Rub. 11. Increase in scholarship by 50% 12. Compensation for food products — 300 /200 Rub., depending on category

Annex 1: continued

Beneficiaries	Benefits before 'monetization'	In-kind benefits remaining in 2005	Cash benefits introduced since 2005
RESPONSIBILITY OF THE FEDERAL BUDGET STARTING FROM 2005			
Judges, prosecutors, tax policemen, customs officers,	1. Death — 180*wage payment 2. Harm to the health — 12* wage payment (if can continue working) — 36* wage payment (if not) 3. Harm to the health (if can not continue working) — monthly compensation= wage-pension. 4. Death — monthly compensation to the dependants= [wage* (# dependants)/(hh. size)]-pension. 5. for judges — urban, suburban and intercity transportation for official proposes 6. for judges after their retirement — compensation for urban, suburban and intercity transportation 7. For judges - accommodation 8. for judges after their retirement (with length of work >=20 years or with disability as a result of working) — in case of moving in other place: separate flat or house. 9. for judges — in special cases (depending on length and place of work) permanent alimony 10. for judges — in special cases (depending on length and place of work) additional paid vacation days 11. for judges and their families — sanatorium-resort therapy	1. for judges — urban, suburban and intercity transportation for official proposes 2. for judges needed accommodation—accommodation. 3. for judges after their retirement (with length of work >=20 years or with disability as a result of working) — in case of moving in other place: separate flat or house. 4. for judges and their families — sanatorium-resort therapy 5. for judges — in special cases (depending on length and place of work) additional paid vacation days	1. Death — 180*wage payment 2. Harm to the health — 12* wage payment (if can continue working) — 36* wage payment (if not) 3. Harm to the health (if can not continue working) — monthly compensation= wage-pension. 4. Death — monthly compensation to the dependants= [wage* (# dependants)/(hh. size)]-pension. 5. for judges after their retirement — compensation for urban, suburban and intercity transportation 6. for judges taking a flat — compensation 7. for judges — in special cases (depending on length and place of work) permanent alimony
RESPONSIBILITY OF THE REGIONAL BUDGETS STARTING FROM 2005			
Veterans of Labor	1. In age of old age pension receiving — denture services 2. Urban, suburban and intercity transportation 3. 50% discount on railroad and water commuter services. 4. 50% discount on housing and utility services 5. 50% discount on solid fuel provision 6. 50% discount on telephone services 7. 50% discount on wired-radio services 8. 50% discount on antenna services	**To be defined by regions of the Russian Federation**	**To be defined by regions of the Russian Federation**

Annex 1: continued

Beneficiaries	Benefits before 'monetization'	In-kind benefits remaining in 2005	Cash benefits introduced since 2005
RESPONSIBILITY OF THE FEDERAL BUDGET STARTING FROM 2005			
Victims of political repressions	1. For rehabilitated — compensation=75 Rub* (#months of imprisonmen) but not more than 10000 Rub. 2. For rehabilitated — seized property or compensations for it (but not more than 400 Rub. for property without dwelling and 10000 Rub. for property with dwelling) 3. For rehabilitated pensioners and disabled —50% discount on provision of medicines 4. For rehabilitated pensioners and disabled — urban, suburban and intercity transportation 5. For rehabilitated pensioners and disabled — railroad and water commuter services. 6. For rehabilitated pensioners and disabled — one time a years two-way ticket on railroad or 50% discount on two-way ticket on water, air services. 7. For rehabilitated pensioners and disabled — 50% discount on housing and utility services 8. For rehabilitated pensioners and disabled — 50% discount on solid fuel provision 9. For rehabilitated pensioners and disabled — free telephone installation 10. For rehabilitated pensioners and disabled — denture services 11. In case of the rehabilitee's death — funeral at the expense of state.	**To be defined by regions of the Russian Federation**	1. For rehabilitated — compensation=75 Rub* (#months of imprisonment) but not more than 10000 Rub. 2. For rehabilitated — seized property or compensations for it (but not more than 400 Rub. for property without dwelling and 10000 Rub. for property with dwelling) **Others to be defined by regions of the Russian Federation**
Home front workers during World War 2	1. No-interest credits for building 2. 50% discount on provision of medicines 3. Denture services 4. Free provision of prosthetic devices 5. Urban, suburban and intercity transportation 6. 50% discount on railroad and water commuter services	**To be defined by regions of the Russian Federation**	**To be defined by regions of the Russian Federation**

Annex 2: The index of monetization.

Assume that region k decides to monetize a certain variety of benefits. Variable p_{jk} corresponds to the k-region' decision to monetize j-benefit.

$$p_{jk} = \begin{cases} 1, & \textit{if region k decides to cash out privilege j} \\ 0, & \textit{if privilege j remains in – kind in region k} \end{cases}$$

The weight of j–benefit will be marked as w_j. Then the monetization index of k-region will be:

$$I_k = 100 \times \sum_{j=1}^{20} w_j \cdot p_{jk} \qquad (1)$$

To determine w_j for each of the 20 benefits the frequency of the regions' decision to monetize it was estimated. The monetization rate of j-benefit was determined as the ratio of N_j (the number of regions who monetize the benefit j), to N, the total number of regions:

$$f_j = \frac{N_j}{N} \qquad (2)$$

If all regions agree to monetize a given benefit j the frequency rate will be 1, but if half of Russian regions monetize it, frequency will be ½, and if none monetize it, the rate will be zero. For practical purposes benefits with the zero monetization rates are excluded from consideration otherwise we will have to deal with the divide-by-zero problem. In our investigation all benefits had positive rates.

As we are interested in rare decisions more, the weight of benefit j will be inversely proportional to the frequency of its monetization:

$$w_l = \frac{C}{f_l} \qquad (3)$$

where C is a normalization coefficient:

$$C = \frac{1}{\sum_{j=1}^{20} \frac{1}{f_l}} \qquad (4)$$

Then with regard for (3) and (4) the weight of j benefit will be:

$$w_j = \frac{1}{f_j \cdot \sum_{l=1}^{20} \frac{1}{f_l}} \qquad (5)$$

Annex 3: Values of monetization index in different regions.

Region name	value of monetization index in	
	December, 2004	April, 2005
Tatarstan	100	100
Tver region	100	100
Vologda region	100	60
Leningrad region	92	23
Tumen region	87	97
Kostroma region	80	39
Kirov region	75	39
Arhangelsk region	60	55
Krasnodarsk territory	60	44
Resp. Komi	60	44
Tomsk region	60	44
Pskov region	60	41
Orel region	58	42
Kemerovskaya obl	.	58
Republic of Bashkiria	.	73
Chita region	.	41
Vladimir region	54	49
Yaroslavl region	50	38
Resp. Mordovia	49	57
Bryansk region	.	37
Tambov region	47	41
Belgorod region	46	29
Nizhny Novgorod region	45	39
Resp. Adigeya	44	36
Ivanovo	44	52
Kaluga region	44	44
Lipetsk region	44	44
Tula region	44	41
Sahalin region	44	7
Resp. Udmurtia	42	56
Sankt–Petersburg	.	42

Annex 3: continued

Region name	value of monetization index in	
	December, 2004	April, 2005
Resp. Kabardino-Balkaria	.	41
Resp. Buryatia	41	0
Hakasiya	.	7
Penza region	39	39
Perm region	39	42
Ryazan region	39	17
Resp Karachaevo-Cherkessia	38	.
Resp Karelia	36	36
Magadan region	.	33
Astrahan region	30	29
Irkutsk region	30	12
Evrey autonomous area	29	39
Kursk region	29	29
Yamalo-Nenets autonomous area	28	100
Primorje territory	.	44
Moscow	.	28
Samara region	27	27
Resp. Tyva	.	27
Resp. Altay	27	27
Murmansk region	.	25
Altay territory	25	23
Orenburg region	25	25
Kamchatka region	.	33
Kaliningrad region	21	24
Moscow region	.	3
Khabarovsk territory	.	0
Novosibirsk region	18	26
Kurgan region	.	44
Saratov region	14	26
Stavropol territory	12	5
Resp.Yakutia (Saha)	.	30

Annex 3: continued

Region name	value of monetization index in	
	December, 2004	April, 2005
Sverdlovsk region	10	7
Resp. Mariy El	10	29
Omsk region	9	35
Smolensk region	8	2
Hanti–Mansi autonomous area	.	15
Resp. Chuvashia	5	0
Resp.Kalmikia	4	4
Ulyanovsk region	.	2
Krasnoyarsk territory	2	21
Rostov region	2	11
Voronezh region	0	44
Volgograd region	0	35
Chelyabinsk region	0	15
Amur region	0	14
Resp. Dagestan	.	3
Chukotska autonomous area	.	0
Resp. North Ossetia	0	0
Novgorod region	0	0

POPULAR REACTIONS TO SOCIAL AND HEALTH SECTOR REFORMS IN RUSSIA'S REGIONS: REFORM VERSUS RETENTION IN SAMARSKAIA AND UL'IANOVSKAIA OBLASTS

ANDREW KONITZER[1]

The breakup of the Soviet Union and the departure by the various republics onto uncertain paths of political and economic transformation brought to an end the soviet-era social contract.[2] As in the former communist countries of Eastern Europe, authorities in the former Soviet states were soon faced with the need to recreate the decaying communist era social safety net in the midst of the new reality of disintegrating central planning and the uneven implementation of market reforms. Policy makers confronted a vastly different political climate than had existed only months before. The prospect of elections loomed as well, with political leaders facing judgment at the hands of a newly-vulnerable constituency.

Among the new postcommunist states, the Russian Federation had its own peculiarities. As a federation, much of the responsibility for the funding and provision of social services was placed upon subnational authorities. Untrained and inexperienced in governing an increasingly market-based society, these authorities faced the dual pressures of pending elections and increasingly tight budget constraints.[3] With no clear set of guidelines to follow in what seemed to be a historically unique situation, the leaders were left to decide on their own how best to maintain a minimum of public order, provide for their constituents and avoid the ire of disgruntled voters at the polls. Their responses varied on a rough continuum, ranging from attempts to maintain substantial elements of the Soviet social contract to efforts to rapidly destroy the old system and rebuild social services and health care provision along the lines of various Western models. The choices bore important ramifications for the health, welfare and social cohesion of the federal subjects.

This paper compares the responses of two administrations in the neighboring regions of Samarskaia and Ul'ianovskaia oblasts, which entered the post-soviet era at roughly the same socio-economic level.[4] In the process, I seek to determine which set of policies was eventually "rewarded" at the polls by regional constituents and which policy packages were best at winning support across different social groups. Through an examination of the social policy paths chosen in each oblast and through an analysis of electoral results after roughly a decade of the chosen reform path, I demonstrate that regional constituencies do seem to respond to both economic performance and social policy outcomes and that regional administrations undertaking more comprehensive reforms may stand a better chance of long-term survival than their counterparts in "slow and steady" regions. In the latter regions, the attempt to retain as much of the old system as possible eventually resulted in the deterioration of social services and the abandonment of the regime by the same vulnerable groups upon which it had initially relied for support.

POPULAR REACTIONS TO SOCIAL SECTOR REFORM

One of the greatest challenges to social reforms within the countries of the Former Soviet Union is to create social programs that reflect the existing financial realities of the post-Soviet milieu while maintaining the political support of a population that is accustomed to comprehensive social protections and can express its level of satisfaction through the ballot box. On the face of things, the task appears intractable. If the broad literature on "economic voting" is correct, then populations tend to utilize retrospective economic evaluations when deciding to sanction incumbent administrations.[5] The initial stages of a postcommunist economic transformation necessarily involved an increase in unemployment, weakening purchasing power and the removal or deterioration of the existing social safety net. Hence, nearly any incumbent identified with these reforms is vulnerable to a popular backlash.

Nonetheless, as Tucker and others have noted, the postcommunist electoral history of Eastern Europe and the former Soviet Union provides mixed evidence for both economic voting and the linkage between social program reform and electoral support.[6] With regard to economic voting, Power and Cox's study of Poland demonstrates that while support for the regime was

apparently affected by attitudes towards economic performance, support
was also partially contingent upon the respondent's perception of whether
the preexisting communist government was to blame for Poland's current
woes.[7] Colton has uncovered relationships between so-called sociotropic
voting and support for incumbent presidents or different political parties in
a series of surveys conducted during the 1995-96 and 1999-2000 Russian
election cycles.[8] Tucker identified a linkage between economic fluctuations and *party type*—a departure from traditional economic voting studies
that focused primarily on attitudes towards the incumbent government.[9]
Turning to the linkage between social welfare reform and voting preferences, Tworzecki found a pattern similar to the one uncovered by Power
and Cox within the realm of economic voting.[10] Here again, voters' attitudes towards material conditions were partially offset by concern over
regime type. Material conditions seem to matter less when voters were considering the possibility of the return to communism in some form, with all
of its implications for democratic governance and liberties.

When considering the reform of social programs within a large federation such as Russia, other factors come into play, which create different incentives and obstacles both for policy makers and the voter. First, because
subnational units operate within a larger federal budget, policy makers in
federal subjects must work within guidelines and constraints established
by federal authorities and are restricted by budgets and tax codes from ac-
quiring additional resources to fund larger social programs. In the 1990s,
poorly defined policy jurisdictions and weak supervision by federal authorities perhaps provided more latitude in Russia for pursuing independent policies than in most federations (as evidenced by both cases). But the
fact remains that an executive would be much harder pressed to preserve
"socialism in one oblast" than "socialism in one country."

Second, voters face different incentives at the regional and local level
than at the national level. Tworzecki found that attitudes towards equality and the welfare state had little impact on Hungarian and Polish elections because individuals' welfare policy preferences were mixed and
often overridden by their attitudes towards the old communist system.
Hence, even if a party did not offer policies that coincided with a voter's
welfare policy preferences, the voter might still support that party based
on its stance towards the old regime. Similar arguments have been used
to explain the success of Boris Yeltsin in 1996.[11] The economic voting

literature would predict a loss for an executive ruling over an economic collapse of Russia's scale, but by portraying the race as a choice between the Yeltsin or the Brezhnev era (or even Stalinist) communism, Yeltsin's campaign team achieved a remarkable victory.

At the subnational level, however, systemic choices are effectively removed from the equation. Because a regional executive is primarily considered to be the region's *khoziain*, or manager, the choice between a liberal or "red" governor will determine the course of socioeconomic policies within that jurisdiction rather than the political principles and institutions that will rule the entire country.[12] In this particular case, because the systemic issue that tended to mask economic or welfare preference voting in many postcommunist cases has been removed, we might expect the danger of voter backlash to be even stronger in the case of the Russian Federation. The only difference is that this backlash would take place primarily at the regional and local levels.[13]

With regional executives largely responsible for the course of social welfare provision during the 1990s, the Russian Federation represented a sort of laboratory where 89 administrations tried their hand at meeting their constituents' needs amid increasingly tight budget constraints. The vote, while certainly subject to a whole array of "administrative resources" and other mechanisms for maintaining executive control over election processes, also altered incentives for a political elite accustomed to operating in a centralized, authoritarian system. Under these conditions, regional executives approached the question of social and economic reform from a range of perspectives which could be crudely grouped into two camps. The first camp viewed "business as usual" (the retention of as much of the old system as possible) as a means to attract the most committed voters and a consistently solid base of political support—pensioners. Often without fully considering how such a system might be funded, executives appealed directly to the elderly and other vulnerable groups and proclaimed themselves to be a bulwark against the corrupt and reckless reforms being emitted from Moscow.

The second camp opted for reform and a clearer break with the soviet social contract. Executives in this camp were certainly aware of the potential for popular backlash but hoped that a rapidly improving regional economy and a growing set of societal "winners" would be sufficient to tip the scales in their favor. Furthermore, an improving economy might provide the necessary budgetary provisions to offer a more solid social safety net than would otherwise be available.

The first camp's strategy was a holding action with few long-term prospects for success, but was perhaps a surer bet for maintaining incumbency in the short term. The second camp's approach was a race against time. If elections occurred before the region experienced improvements in the economy, incumbents could face a very challenging election. For both, the novelty of the post-Soviet experience and the mixed signals emitted from postcommunist Eastern Europe provided few guidelines. Which approach would best yield the necessary popular support to retain office?

To preserve or dismantle?

Throughout the 1990s, Samarskaia oblast's Governor Konstantin Titov and Ul'ianovskaia oblast's Governor Iurii Goriachev exhibited a remarkable contrast in leadership styles, ideology and bases for legitimacy that neatly reflected the two approaches to social policy and economic reform discussed above.[14] Goriachev was appointed to office in 1992, and promised to shelter the region's population from the perceived ravages of Yegor Gaidar's reforms through a measured retreat from the remnants of the old social contract and "slow and steady" market reforms.[15] In neighboring Samarskaia oblast, the Titov administration attempted to rapidly dismantle the remnants of the old social guarantees and to restructure the region's economic and social service sectors.

Promising to provide protection against "*urrah* democrats," shock-therapy liberals and criminals, Goriachev cultivated a solid core of support as a "defender" of vulnerable sectors within the oblast. One of the administration's first actions was to soften the blow of price liberalization during the winter of 1992. The oblast concluded contracts with firms that had been transferred into the hands of individuals drawn from, or allying themselves with, the governor's ruling clique.[16] Through barter and partially monetarized exchanges, these firms provided food and other essential goods to consumers at some of the lowest prices in the Russian Federation.[17] In another practice reminiscent of the centralized economy, firms in the region provided many goods and services to the oblast social services department. Agricultural enterprises also played a key role in this process. Through a system of *tovarnii kredit*,[18] farmers and farm enterprises received a range of material inputs in exchange for selling portions of their harvest to the administration at below market prices.[19]

During the initial stages of reform in neighboring Samarskaia oblast, authorities took little action to shield the region's citizenry from the pain of price liberalization and the breakdown of central planning. The Titov administration, building its support from among local industrialists in the energy and banking sector, small and medium *biznesmeni*, and other working age citizens and students not tied to weapons production and other traditional industries, sought to overcome the difficulties of the post-Soviet economy by promoting new business growth and encouraging outside investment. A perusal of regional press accounts from the early 1990s indicates that Titov treated economic restructuring and liberalization as an imperative—the only means to escape Russia's socio-economic woes.

Such policies succeeded in attracting a comparatively large amount of outside investment (including foreign capital) to the region and drove the steady development of new forms of economic activity that gradually offset the worst effects from the decline of the region's military industrial and aerospace complex. Throughout the second half of the 1990s, Samarskaia oblast consistently appeared amongst the top ten regions in a variety of economic performance indicators. In terms of finance, by 1996, Samarskaia oblast was an established "donor" region[20] and after 1998, the region boasted one of the federation's few balanced regional budgets.

An examination of wage dynamics in the two regions provides perhaps the most succinct means to assess the immediate and long-term effects of these alternative socio-economic policies on the working population's standard of living. In the early 1990s, a comparison of wages adjusted to the regional costs of living (*prozhitochnyi minimum*) indicated that workers' incomes, while lower in absolute terms in Ul'ianovskaia oblast than in Samarskaia oblast, yielded substantially greater purchasing power in the former region. This reflected the impact of Goriachev's price controls and other subsidization policies. Ul'ianovskaia oblast maintained this margin over its neighbor until roughly 1995-1996, when increasing wages in Samarskaia oblast, along with the collapse of many social guarantees in Ul'ianovskaia oblast, gave Samarskaia oblast's workers comparatively greater purchasing power. After 1996, Samarskaia oblast's workers continued to pull steadily away from their counterparts in Ul'ianovskaia oblast.[21]

In terms of health care and regional social programs, the two administrations again chose markedly different paths. In Ul'ianovskaia oblast (operating in line the premise: "in medicine, you need a strong vertical administration") the Goriachev administration took every step to essentially preserve the health care system as it had existed during the Soviet era. Ignoring federal guidelines for the provision of health insurance, the region only assigned policies to workers, and then proceeded to finance the health care system through direct payments from the oblast budget. Funds continued to be distributed according to the size of the facility in question and the administration was often criticized for manipulating the flow of resources for its own political gain. Inevitably, this wasteful approach, which largely ignored the actual cost of services provided, resulted in shortages and wage arrears. Unlike Samarskaia oblast, the Ul'ianovskaia oblast administration discouraged the development of private care facilities and other forms of paid services. In fact, the administration-controlled media attacked private care facilities because they supposedly served the needs of the wealthy and corrupt with which the Goriachev administration was ostensibly always in conflict.[22]

Centralization in Ul'ianovskaia oblast brought additional problems, since substantial funds passed under the control of individuals who were subject to very little public oversight. In 1995, an investigation by federal authorities resulted in a shake-up at the region's Territorial Obligatory Health Insurance Fund (TFOMS), with charges ranging from mere incompetence to fraud and embezzlement. The report cited extremely high wages for personnel, payments to local firms of sums disproportionate to the services and goods provided, and the use of insurance money to cover services and facilities that lay outside the federally mandated responsibilities of the regional health insurance system.[23]

Samarskaia oblast stood at the vanguard of health service reform throughout the 1990s. As one of the territories chosen for a late-Soviet era experiment in health care cost accounting called the "new economic mechanism," Samarskaia oblast entered the post-Soviet period with a significant advantage in terms of knowledge and experience in health care reform. In December 1993, the region became the first in the federation to fully implement Russia's new mandatory health insurance system. The region made great advances in the training and promotion of general practice doctors and, by 2000, it boasted one-third of all such specialists in the Russian Federation. Other cost saving advances where made in the development of outpatient services and day clinics where Samarskaia oblast once again stood at the forefront in terms of the number of patients receiving less expensive outpatient treatment. Private care services were also actively promoted and citizens in Samarskaia oblast soon had a relatively wide range of choice in terms of the quality and type of care. Finally, a strong pharmaceutical market backed by administration-supported services (which kept consumers informed about the cost and characteristics of different products) increased the availability and reduced the cost of medicine. As a result, in 2000, the cost of medicine in the region was 2 percent lower than the federal average.

Table 1: Comparison of Healthcare Budgets[24]

	Samarskaia oblast 1998		Ul'ianovskaia oblast 1998		Samarskaia oblast 2000		Ul'ianovskaia oblast 2000	
	% Total Exp.[a]	Rubles[b] per Capita	% Total Exp.[a]	Rubles[b] per Capita	% Total Exp.[a]	Rubles[b] per Capita	% Total Exp.[a]	Rubles[b] per Capita
Total Budget Expenditures	—	2864.90	—	1536.11	—	3563.81	—	1872.41
Total Health Expenditures	15.6	446.74	22.4	344.63	14.7	522.02	29.7	556.39
Including:								
Personnel	1.5	6.75	31.2	107.53	1.6	8.28	31.9	117.28
Supplies	0.4	1.97	15.6	53.85	0.5	2.42	18.0	100.32
Food	0.2	1.01	9.0	31.05	0.3	1.79	7.9	43.76
Equipment	1.7	7.75	2.5	8.65	1.6	8.29	1.6	8.82
Construction	8.3	37.29	8.3	28.69	8.4	43.85	5.8	32.43
"Other"	87.7	391.97	33.3	114.87	87.6	457.40	34.8	193.77

[a] Figures in the "Total Health Expenditures" row indicate the precentage of total budget expenditures devoted to health care. For the health care budget items (all rows below "including"), the figures indicate the precentage of total health care expenditures devoted to each item.

[b] Exchange rates: December 31, 1998—20.65 rubles/dollar; December 31, 2000—28.86 rubles/dollar

A brief comparison of the total health expenditures in Samarskaia oblast and Ul'ianovskaia oblast provides a relatively objective illustration of the functioning of each region's health care system. For both 1998 and 2000, the portion of Samarskaia oblast's consolidated budget devoted to health care was roughly 15 percent. In neighboring Ul'ianovskaia oblast, health care consumed over 22 percent of the total budget in 1998, and nearly 30 percent in 2000. Two factors account for these outcomes. First, as noted in the table, Samarskaia oblast enjoyed significantly higher budget revenues in both years. Another factor contributing to this outcome was the greater inefficiency of Ul'ianovskaia oblast's health care system. A breakdown of the total expenditures illustrates this point. Expenditures for wages to "personnel" (defined below) accounted for between 1.5 percent and 1.6 percent (6.75–8.28 rubles per capita) of the total health budget in Samarskaia oblast, while in Ul'ianovskaia oblast, the same category consumed nearly one-third (107.54 – 177.28 rubles per capita) of all health budget expenditures during both years. [25] Similar differences persisted across other categories, with the exception of new construction and equipment purchases, which drew either an equivalent percentage in both regions' budgets or a larger portion of Samarskaia oblast's. Samarskaia oblast's large (over 87 percent of total health expenditures) "other" category is in fact an indication of a health care budget working according to the existing federal standards. This category represents funds directed toward the payment of services for the uninsured and underinsured.

These marked disparities indicate another significant difference between the two regions' health care finance policies. Samarskaia oblast's health care budget demonstrates the oblast's implementation of a "single channel" health care finance system. According to the normative scheme for health insurance provision in the regions, insurance companies are to cover the costs of both the employed and unemployed, with the oblast budget making payments for the policies of the latter group; the vast majority of financing passes through the TFOMS. The volume of budget finances falling into Samarskaia oblast's "other category" represents the portion of budget funds diverted to cover policies for the non-working sector of the population, as well as underpayment by enterprises for their workers' policies. In accordance with federal laws, TFOMS funds cover most wages, medicine, food and supplies. Ul'ianovskaia oblast's budget represents the type of partially institutionalized "dual channel" system that existed in many regions. The

Ul'ianovskaia oblast TFOMS covered a portion of both the employed and unemployed, but the oblast budget paid for only a portion of the policies for the latter. At the same time, a portion of the payments for practitioners' and administrators' wages, medicine, supplies, and food pass directly from the oblast budget to regional medical institutions. The dual channel system results in additional waste from the added bureaucratic costs, redundancy and questionable accounting procedures.[26]

The situation surrounding the social services sector in Ul'ianovskaia oblast echoed some of the problems within the region's health care system. Throughout the 1990s, and in accordance with the Goriachev administration's "slow transition to the market," the administration continued to direct much of the region's budget towards the payment of energy, transport and food subsidies. These untargeted programs essentially wasted resources on individuals who could otherwise afford to pay, and thus reduced the finances available to provide quality goods and services for the needy.[27]

Short on "live money," the administration resorted to barter and an extensive network of volunteer organizations.[28] With regard to the first, various firms provided essential goods such as medicine and food, UAZ sent vehicles directly from the plant to social service institutions, and construction firms contributed materials for the construction of facilities. In some instances, barter met the needs of both local firms and the regional government. However, the demonetarization of the system contributed to the region's budget revenue problems and left decision makers with the constant headache of converting bartered goods into resources proper to the task in question.

The Goriachev administration's bid for the support of the elderly population resulted in a relatively advantageous position for this sector of society. Interviews with social services staff members and the head of the city of Ul'ianovsk's social services department indicated a marked emphasis on programs oriented toward pensioners and invalids. In addition to a host of clubs and activities, the oblast hosted a unique system of spas and sanatoriums where the elderly, veterans and invalids could meet, take part in social activities, and receive various non-traditional treatments. However, indications of the region's dire financial straits appeared even around these showcases of regional social policy. As the head of the city of Ul'ianovsk's social services department indicated, "we need to use non-traditional methods because we lack the money for anything else. If we can't afford to treat or cure ailments, we at least try to make the elderly feel comfortable and happy."[29]

Furthermore, if the region focused a significant portion of its scarce resources on the elderly, one could not say the same for the young. Child welfare, an area for which regions bore complete financial responsibility, was subject to chronic arrears and underpayment (see a comparison of child welfare expenditures in Table 2). Throughout the decade, the oblast administration had attempted to offset insufficient cash payments through practices of barter and payments in kind. This might include reductions in apartment fees, or free essential goods and services from local firms to the neediest families. Nonetheless, arrears steadily increased. In March 2000, the administration claimed that it would begin steady payments, starting with dues owed from the previous month. However, in practice this once again applied only to the neediest families—single parent households, invalid and underage parents, and large families in which the per member income dropped below that of the current poverty level. At the time, there were 250,000 children in the oblast who were eligible for child welfare payments and the oblast's new plan would not cover anywhere near this number.[30]

The performance of Samarskaia oblast's social service sector (see Table 2 for a comparison of budget expenditures) indicates the importance of balancing economic performance and public goods provision. For most of the 1990s, Samarskaia oblast's administration consistently met its obligations in terms of unemployment and child welfare payments while guaranteeing pensions and gradually expanding a set of additional social services. Although efficiency gains wrought by the administration's avoidance of such untargeted programs (such as high subsidies to the energy, housing and transportation sectors) partly assisted in achieving these outcomes, interviews with oblast administration officials consistently pointed to a more mundane contributing factor: better economic performance was due to higher budget revenues. Samarskaia oblast's focus on new business development, while initially yielding detrimental residual effects on social welfare in the form of unemployment in traditional sectors and an overall higher cost of living, eventually yielded sufficient financial resources to ensure that the administration met its social service obligations (hence the significant margin of Samarskaia oblast's overall social service expenditures over Ul'ianovskaia oblast's. See Table 2).[31]

Table 2: Comparison of Social Policy Budgets

	Samarskaia oblast 1998		Ul'ianovskaia oblast 1998		Samarskaia oblast 2000		Ul'ianovskaia oblast 2000	
	% Total Exp.[a]	Rubles per Capita	% Total Exp.[a]	Rubles per Capita	% Total Exp.[a]	Rubles per Capita	% Total Exp.[a]	Rubles per Capita
Total Social Service Expenditures	10.6	302.71	7.4	113.69	13.7	488.19	6.1	113.27
Including:								
Soc. Servant Wages	8.0	24.13	7.0	7.95	6.6	32.35	10.1	11.40
Medical Products	0.5	1.50	0.2	0.27	0.6	2.75	0.1	0.09
Food	3.0	9.05	4.5	5.07	2.2	10.79	7.0	7.96
Equipment	1.5	4.60	0.1	0.07	0.5	2.65	0.0	0.00
Construction	0.9	2.56	0.5	0.55	0.8	4.06	0.5	0.57
Child Welfare	47.3	143.15	43.6	49.57	19.1	93.39	40.2	45.55

[a] Figures in the "Total Social Service Expenditures" row indicate the percentage of total budget expenditures devoted to social services. For the social service budget items (all rows below "including"), the figures indicate the percentage of total social services expenditures devoted to each item. As with the health care figures, these items do not sum to 100 percent of expenditures. In this case, the substantial remainder primarily represents expenditures for specific social programs (like Samarskaia oblast's pension supplements) not represented in the federal level data. For total budget expenditures see Table 1.

Perhaps the most publicized example of the Samarskaia oblast administration's success in balancing economic development with public goods provision came in the autumn of 1999 when Governor Titov challenged federal authorities over the size of regional pensions. The scandal began with the federal government's failure to implement the July 21, 1997 federal law, "On the procedures for calculating and increasing state pensions," which required an increase in the coefficient between the state minimal pension and the official average wage from .525 to .7. Despite this legislation, the federal government continued to pay out pensions at the previous, lower coefficient of .525.[32] On October 13, 1999, Governor

Titov delivered a decree, in which he stated that pensions in Samarskaia oblast would be paid according to the .7 coefficient, and that the extra funds needed to finance this increase would be drawn from surplus payments into the region's pension fund.[33] This decree drew an immediate response from the General Prosecutor who stated that the oblast administration had no right to redistribute federal resources. A very public confrontation ensued after which the governor conceded to federal authorities and stopped drawing money from Samarskaia oblast's pension fund surplus. Nonetheless, the oblast continued to pay out pensions according to the .7 coefficient, with additional funds drawn directly from the regional budget.[34]

Titov's struggle with the federal government was probably noisier than necessary.[35] Pensioners received their monthly payments according to the lower coefficient for nearly two years, and the Samarskaia oblast administration only took action on the eve of a Titov's ill-fated 2000 presidential bid. Even so, it had its intended effect: increasing the governor's popularity among the sector of society that traditionally opposed the type of reforms that the administration undertook. Furthermore, while nothing could save Titov's bid for the presidency in March 2000, increased support among pensioners played an important role in his re-election as governor in July.[36] A strong economy gave Titov the means to implement populist policies, if necessary, for his political survival. In contrast, financial constraints prevented Ul'ianovskaia oblast's administration from even contemplating a similar move.

To borrow Mustard's formulation, the Samarskaia oblast administration struck a more effective balance between development in the "real economy" and the provision of health and social services.[37] Oblast authorities made efforts to enhance the investment climate and attract business with openly liberal development policies. At the same time, the administration reduced costs in the social and health sectors and promoted the development of private and non-profit sector alternatives for the state's divested responsibilities. The result was a comparatively more efficient and self-sustaining system. Greater economic performance produced the budget revenues necessary to finance the region's leaner social and health services sectors and resulted in the more or less full provision of those goods and services that the state continued to guarantee. Simply put, Samarskaia oblast's administration promised less than its counterparts in Ul'ianovskaia oblast, but due to a combination of the above listed factors, actually delivered more.

Popular Reactions

Popular reactions to the two chosen reform paths in these neighboring oblasts provide important insights into the potential success of regional-level social program reforms within the Russian Federation. The results of each region's 2000 regional executive elections give us some sense of their respective publics' responses to the two approaches—Governor Titov handily won the 2000 election in a single election round, while Governor Goriachev lost by a large margin to his opponent Vladimir Shamanov.[38] Both election campaigns were run as popular referenda on the course of reforms undertaken in the two oblasts over the past decade, and there were even occasional comparisons in the media (especially in Ul'ianovskaia oblast) between the outcomes in the neighboring regions. Among local pundits, the results of the contests were interpreted largely in terms of the success (Titov) and failure (Goriachev) of the chosen reform paths.

However, aggregate level outcomes provide insufficient bases on which to draw conclusions about which types of individuals supported each incumbent. Survey data drawn prior to the two regions' 2000 regional executive elections allows us to better explore the micro-level decisions that produced these electoral results.[39] The primary question is to determine which policies resulted in the greatest polarization between social groups and also to identify which groups in society were particularly dissatisfied with the course of the regime's socio-economic programs. To examine this question, I ran logistic regression models including age, employment status (a categorical variable), gender, education and personal material status as predictors for incumbent support. Because the policies in Samarskaia oblast appear to have provided more effective social service provision as well as opportunities for the working portion of the population, I expect the socio-economic predictors to account for less variance in support for governor Titov than for governor Goriachev. To take age as an example, a distribution of public goods across all age groups would yield more equal support across the different age categories and make this variable a poor predictor of regime support. However, a regime that focuses its efforts more on the elderly would create a situation in which one could better predict support for the candidate by looking at the respondent's age.

For the most part, the results of the analysis bore out these predictions. Models which examined the linkage between the respondent's age, work status (student, pensioner, unemployed, working), education and material situation in both regions were significantly better at predicting support for Iurii Goriachev than for Konstantin Titov. The Ul'ianovskaia oblast model resulted in a pseudo R^2 of 0.10 while the Samarskaia oblast model yielded a pseudo R^2 of only 0.02. This indicates that there was significantly more disagreement among social groups over support for the regime and its policies in Ul'ianovskaia oblast than in Samarskaia oblast, and also suggests that resources and opportunities were better distributed in the latter region.

Figure 1: Changes in Probability of Supporting the Incumbent Across Age Catgories[40]

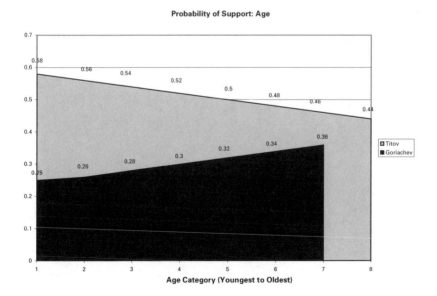

Looking more closely at the breakdown of support across different groups, in lieu of the more traditional method of presenting a
table of logistic regression coefficients, I present graphical representa-
tions of the changes in the probability of supporting either Governor
Goriachev or Governor Titov for respondents in different social categories. While interpreting the tables, the reader can treat the numbers as the percentage likelihood that a respondent in each category
(holding all other categories at their mean) would support the incumbent in question. Figure 1 shows the change in probability of support as one moves across different age categories. The pattern clearly
demonstrates the different dynamics of support resulting from the
policy choices in each region and also indicates that, in this particular
case the difference in the probability of supporting Titov between
the youngest and oldest age groups is greater than in Ul'ianovskaia
oblast (14 points as opposed to Ul'ianovskaia oblast's 11 points).
Nonetheless, we see that the oldest age category in Samarskaia oblast
was still more likely to support the incumbent than the oldest age
category in Ul'ianovskaia oblast.

Figure 2 presents the differences in probabilities of support for pensioners versus non-pensioners. As we might expect, the differences in the probabilities of support across these two groups is greater in the Ul'ianovskaia oblast case than in the Samaraskaia oblast. Surprisingly, we also see that pensioners were more likely to support the incumbent in *both* regions. Most likely this reflects the success of the Titov administration in attracting pensioners after his standoff over the pension coefficient in 1999.

Figure 2: Probability of Supporting the Incumbents Among Pensioners and Non-pensioners

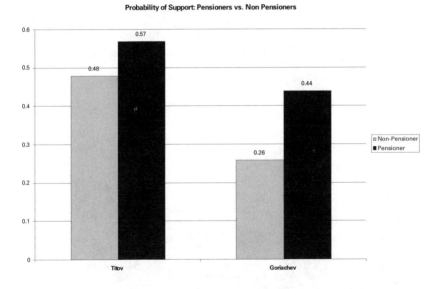

Probability of Support: Pensioners vs. Non Pensioners

Moving on to figure 3, we see changes in the probability of supporting each incumbent as one moves from the respondent's lowest self-assessment of his or her economic situation to the highest self-assessment. In this instance the figures indicate that, despite the markedly different social programs undertaken in each region, the poorest were still the least likely to support *both* governors, and the differences between the poorest and the best-off are roughly the same across the two regions. Despite Goriachev's image as defender of the poor and misfortunate, it appears that the relatively better off were just as likely to support the regime—and the poorer to oppose it —in both regions. Furthermore, we once again see that the least well off in Samarskaia oblast were still more likely to support the incumbent than in Ul'ianovskaia oblast.

Figure 3: Probability of Supporting the Incumbent Across Different Economic Self Assessments[41]

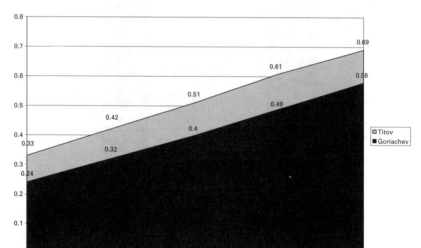

Probability of Support: Personal Material Assessment

Economic Self Assessment (lowest to highest)

Finally, we turn to different probabilities of support across levels of education. In this instance we see a marked difference in the variance of support across the two regions and a clear indication that Goriachev had alienated the best educated through policies that failed to support disloyal educational institutions and lowered job opportunities for those most likely to benefit from a stronger economy.

Figure 4: Probability of Supporting the Incumbent Across Different Educational Categories[42]

Probability of Support: Education

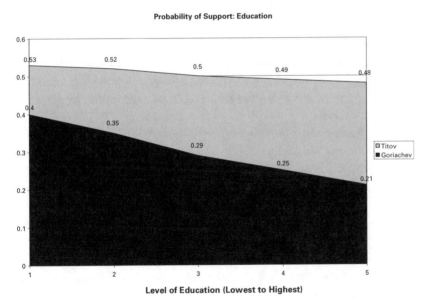

Level of Education (Lowest to Highest)

To sum up the results presented in this section, it appears that the policies pursued in Samarskaia oblast were much more successful in garnering support across a wider range of the electorate. The pattern of support in each region generally followed expectations, and Titov's ability to deliver both jobs and social services appears to have won broad-based support. By choosing to transform the local economy and social services, the Titov administration had successfully balanced the working and non-working sectors of society and possessed the resources to attract the votes of even those groups that are traditionally in opposition to the type of liberal reforms undertaken in the region during the 1990s.

CONCLUSIONS

Developments in Samarskaia and Ul'ianovskaia oblasts offer an indication of the degree to which post-Soviet approaches to the provision of social and health services can vary from region to region and how these outcomes might impact popular support for different regimes. In Ul'ianovskaia oblast, the administration's rhetoric of social guarantees and protection from the ravages of the market conflicted with the realities of the region's bloated and poorly managed health and social sectors. The elderly population received the most benefits while the administration alienated the educated, young and working age sectors of society—the very groups responsible for supporting the system's main beneficiaries.

Better quality, more broadly distributed public goods and employment opportunities in Samarskaia oblast created wide-based political support for an outwardly liberal regime. While vulnerable groups in society faced higher prices for basic goods and services, a growing economy—buoyed by outside investment, leaner and more effective social and health care services, and a rising NGO and private care sector—gave substance to social services, which in other regions existed only on paper. At the same time, the working sector in Samarskaia oblast experienced increases in wages and opportunities, which exceeded those of their counterparts in Ul'ianovskaia oblast. Finally, the additional resources made available by leaner social and health services and a larger tax base provided additional "crisis" resources to carry the oblast administration through various political challenges. In an ironic twist, it was Konstantin Titov, rather than Iurii Goriachev who could resort to pre-election boosts in social spending in order to carry the 2000 elections—liberal reforms had provided the luxury of increased revenues, and therefore the option for short-term populist strategies.[43]

From the policy perspective, a number of important potential lessons may be drawn from these cases. First, decentralization of responsibilities may serve the dual purposes of tailoring policies for regional needs and providing a clearer target for voters to focus their satisfaction or dissatisfaction with standard of living issues. Decentralization in a postcommunist setting can both reduce pressures on national leaders pursuing macro changes in political and economic systems and force subnational policymakers to focus more on the immediate needs of their citizenry. In some respects, such a situation prevents standard of living issues from derailing attempts to dismantle authoritarian or centrally planned systems at the national level while still providing a safety valve for material concerns at the subnational level.

Secondly, the cases demonstrate that social safety nets can be dismantled without necessarily endangering the political tenure of policy makers. Pursued at the subnational level, the "slow and steady" approach is a short-term solution that will eventually lead to broad-based dissatisfaction with the regime, as infrastructure deteriorates and the resources necessary to support a poorly-targeted social safety net dry up. Goriachev survived one election on the support of a narrow sector of society that had enjoyed extensive social programs at the expense of the region's economic future. A decade of cannibalizing the region and mortgaging future development eventually exhausted available resources and led to the collapse of those programs targeted toward Goriachev's main base of support. In this respect, "backlash" was delayed only to destroy the regime during the 2000 election.

In Samarskaia oblast, Titov's regime managed to strike a balance between economic development and the provision of social services. A leaner social and health sector demanded less budgetary resources and was less of a draw on the regional economy. As the region experienced an economic upturn starting in the mid-1990s, the increased tax base created surpluses, which allowed the regime to periodically pursue populist policies and eventually attract sufficient support—even from pensioners and other traditional opponents of liberal reforms.[44]

A two-case comparison is an inadequate basis to make a definitive conclusion regarding the necessary policies to reform postcommunist social systems while avoiding voter backlash. However, the cases of Samarskaia and Ul'ianovskaia oblasts raise interesting questions that challenge some of the preconceived notions regarding such reforms. Further research including more cases would help better illuminate some of the patterns suggested above and provide a stronger basis upon which to build policy prescriptions.

ENDNOTES

1. Materials for this analysis were collected during a year of field research in Samarskaia oblast and Ul'ianovskaia oblast from August 2000 to August 2001. Financial assistance for this research was provided by an Institute of International Education (IIE) Professional Development Fellowship and the ACTR/ACCELS Regional Scholar Exchange Program. I wish to thank all the members of the Study Group on Social Cohesion for their comments on earlier versions of this manuscript. Special thanks also go to Lidia Goverdovskaia, Igor Yegorov and Valentin Bazhanov for arranging contacts with regional officials in Samarskaia oblast and Ul'ianovskaia oblast. The points expressed in this paper are my own and do not necessarily represent the positions of IIE, ACTR/ACCELS, or the Carnegie Corporation.

2. For details about the Soviet social contract see: Linda Cook, *The Soviet Social Contract and Why it Failed: Welfare Policy and Workers' Politics from Brezhnev to Yeltsin*, (Cambridge: Harvard University Press, 1993).

3. However, as some works fiscal federal relations have shown, the budget constraints on regional administrations were still much "softer" than those in other advanced industrial federations. See: Daniel Treisman, "The Politics of Soft Credit in Russia," *Europe-Asia Studies*, 47 (1995): 949-976; Darrell Slider, "Russia's Market-Distorting Federalism," *Post-Soviet Geography and Economics*, 38 (1997): 445-460.

4. According to data from 1999, Samarskaia oblast had a population of 3,294,000 situated on 53.6 thousand square kilometers of territory. Approximately 80% of the region's population lived in urban settlements, and manufacturing constituted the largest economic sector, employing 27.5% of the working population. The region historically maintained a reputation for its aerospace and weapons factories, the AvtoVAZ auto plant (supplying roughly 75% of all domestic Russian auto production), chemical production, and oil and gas extraction and refinement. However, by 2000, the aerospace and weapons production industry was a shadow of its former self and production related to the AvtoVAZ plant remained the core of the economy.

In 1999, Ul'ianovskaia oblast's population stood at 1,463,200 people situated across 37.2 thousand square kilometers of territory. 73.1% of the population lived in urban settlements and, similar to Samarskaia oblast, manufacturing approximately 1/3rd of the working population. Like its neighbor, Ul'ianovskaia oblast was also recognized for its aerospace, weapons and automobile manufacturing (UAZ). While both weapons and aircraft production had decreased in importance, Ul'ianovskaia oblast's Aviastar aircraft production facility remained relatively active. In terms of other types of production, Ul'ianovskaia oblast featured a weak oil and gas sector, but maintained some chemical production. Construction companies also played a large role in the regional economy. Data drawn from Samarskaia Oblast Committee of State Statistics, *Samarskaia Oblast-99: Statisticheskii sbornik* (Samara: Samarskaia Oblast Committee of state Statistics,

2000); Ul'ianovskaia Oblast Committee of State Statistics, *Ekonomicheskoe polozhenie Ul'ianvoskoi Oblasti v 1999 godu* (Ul'ianovsk: Ul'ianovskaia Oblast Committee
of state Statistics, 2000)

5. Gerald Kramer, "Short-Term Fluctuations in U.S. Voting Behavior,
1896–1964," *American Political Science Review* 65 (1971): 131–43; Howard Bloom
and Douglas Price, "Voter Response to Short-Run Economic Conditions:
The Asymmetric Effect of Prosperity and Recession," *American Political Science
Review* 69 (1975): 1240–54; Edward Tufte, "Determinants of the Outcomes of
Midterm Congressional Elections," *American Political Science Review* 69 (1975):
812–26; Edward Tufte, *Political Control of the Economy* (Princeton, N.J.: Princeton
University Press, 1978); Raymond Fair, "The Effects of Economic Events on
Votes for the President," *Review of Economics and Statistics* 60 (1978): 159–73; J. R.
Hibbing and J. R. Alford, "The Electoral Impact of Economic Conditions: Who
Is Held Responsible?" *American Journal of Political Science* 25 (1981): 423–39; Kinder
and Kiewiet, "Sociotropic Politics"; Stanley Feldman, "Economic Self-Interest and
Political Behavior," *American Journal of Political Science* 26 (1982): 446–66; Stephen
Weatherford, "Economic Conditions and Electoral Outcomes: Class Differences
in the Political Response to Recession," *American Journal of Political Science* 22
(1983): 917–38; Morris Fiorina, "Economic Retrospective Voting in American
National Elections: A Micro-Analysis," *American Journal of Political Science* 22
(1978): 426–43.

6. Joshua Tucker, "Reconsidering Economic Voting: Party Type vs.
Incumbency in Transition Countries," Paper presented at the Annual Meeting of
the American Political Science Association, Atlanta GA., September 1999.

7. Powers, D.V. and J.H. Cox, *Echoes from the Past: The Relationship between
Satisfaction with Economic Reforms and Voting Behavior in Poland.* American Political
Science Review, 1997. 91(3): 617-633.

8. Timothy Colton, "Economics and Voting in Russia," *Post-Soviet Affairs* 12
(1996): 313-314; Timothy Colton, *Transitional Citizens: Voters and What Influences
Them in the New Russia* (Cambridge: Harvard University Press, 2000); Timothy
Colton and Michael McFaul, *Popular Choice and Managed Democracy* (Washington
DC: Brookings Institution Press, 2003)

9. Tucker, J.A., *Transitional Economic Voting: Economic Conditions and Election
Results in Russia, Poland, Hungary, Slovakia, and the Czech Republic from 1990-1999.*
2004: Princeton, Michigan.

10. Hubert Tworzeski, "Welfare-State Atttitudes and Electoral Outcomes in
Hungary," *Problems of Post-Communism*, 47:6 (2000): 17-28.

11. David Mason and Svetlana Sidorenko-Stephenson, "Public Opinion and the
1996 Elections in Russia: Nostolgic and Statist, Yet Pro-Market and Pro-Yeltsin,"
Slavic Review, 56:4 (1997): 698-717.

12. Studies of so-called second-order elections in Europe indicate that voters
face markedly different incentives in "first order" (central) than in second order
(regional) elections. See Karlheinz Reif, "Ten Second-Order National Elections,"

in *Ten European Elections*, ed. Karleinz Reif (Aldershot, U.K.: Gower Publishing, 1985), 1–36; Pippa Norris, "Second Order Elections Revisited," *European Journal of Political Research*, 31 (1997) 109–14; Karleinz Reif, "European Elections as Member State Second-Order Elections Revisited, *European Journal of Political Research* 31 (1997), 115–24; Michael Marsh, "Testing the Second-Order Election Model after Four European Elections," *British Journal of Politics* 29 (1998): 591–607.

13. For evidence of economic voting at the regional level, see Andrew Konitzer, *Voting for Russia's Governors: Regional Elections and Accountability Under Yeltsin and Putin*, (Baltimore: Johns Hopkins University Press, forthcoming 2005); Andrew Konitzer-Smirnov, "Serving Different Masters: Regional Executives and Accountability in Ukraine and Russia," *Europe-Asia Studies*, 57:1, 2005; Andrew Konitzer-Smirnov, "Jurisdictional Voting in Russia's Regions: Initial Results from Individual-level Analyses," *Europe-Asia Studies*, 55:1, 2003.

14. Materials for this section were gathered from regional press materials, interviews, and other sources in Samarskaia oblast and Ul'ianovskaia oblast. Arbakhan Magamedov's contribution to Hokkaido University's "Regionii Rossii: Khronika i rukovoditeli" provided a useful guide for navigating post-Soviet events in Ul'ianovskaia oblast. See: Magamedov, A., "Khronika politicheskii sobytii" in *Regionii Rossii: Khronika i rukovoditeli. Tom 6: Nizhegorodskaia oblast, Ul'ianovskaia oblast*, eds K. Matsuzato and A. Shatilov (Sapporo: Hokkaido University Slavic Research Center, 1999).

15. I emphasize the term "remnants" to denote the degree to which the social guarantees undergirding the Soviet social contract had deteriorated even prior to the collapse of the Soviet Union. Once again, see: Cook, 1993.

16. Ul'ianovskkhlebtorg, (the regional bread monopoly) provides one of the clearest examples of this type of collusion. In a unique chapter in the history of Russian privatization, the region's entire bread industry was "privatized" into a single joint stock company that held a monopoly over all bread production in the region. In exchange, the firm supplied inexpensive bread to the population that, despite promises of full subsidization, was only partially financed by the oblast administration (Oleg Samartsev, interview with author, Ul'ianovsk, Ul'ianovskaia oblast, 3 November 2000).

17. The Soviet coupon system also continued to operate for a number of goods and good categories until at least 1996.

18. Literally - "goods credit"

19. Igor Yegorov, series of interviews with author, Ul'ianovsk, Ul'ianovskaia oblast, Autumn 2000.

20. A donor region is one whose contributions to the federal budget are in excess of the federal funds returned to the region. In 1996, only nine regions of Russia's 89 were official "donors." See Avtandil Tsuladze, "Tri pravitel'stva – tri istochnika protivorichii" *Segodnia Online* 28 June 2000. 10 December 2001 <http://www.7days.ru/w3s.nsf/Archive/2000_164_polit_text_culadze1.html>

21. See: Goskomstat Rossii, *Regionii Rossii: 2000* (Moscow: Goskomstat, 2000) and Goskomstat Rossii, *Regionii Rossii: 1998* (Moscow: Goskomstat, 1998).

22. Gennadii Iakimchev, "Aleksandr Nabegaev provali, pervoe zadanie" *Simbirskii Kur'er*, 11 April 2000.

23. L. Makarova, "V poiskakh rastrachennogo...," *Simbirskii Kur'er*, 19 October, 1995.

24. Health and social services budget data for this study was provided by Dr. Aleksei Lavrov of the Russian Ministry of Finance. Figures represent actual budget execution (data was extracted by standardized forms completed by each region) and is therefore not subject to the implementation issues arising from the use of published budget laws. Space considerations limited the number and choice of years. By presenting figures from 1998 and 2000, I demonstrate the long-term effects of policies implemented during the beginning of the decade. The use of nonconsecutive years indicates the consistency of the differences illustrated in the tables.

25. In per capita terms, expenditures on wages in Ul'ianovskaia oblast were roughly 16 (1998) to 21 times (2000) greater than of Samarskaia oblast. Per capita budgetary expenditures on medicine in Ul'ianovskaia oblast were roughly 27 and 41 times greater, and food products drew per capita expenditures of 31 (1998) to 24 (2000) times those of Samarskaia oblast.

26. Mikhail Zasypkin, interview with author, tape recording, Samara, Samarskaia oblast, Russia, 26 June 2001. Judyth Twigg also offered assistance in interpreting these figures.

27. The cost of tickets on Ul'ianovskaia oblast's transport was largely frozen for much of the 1990s. By the winter of 2001, broken heaters, frozen doors, and complete shutdowns were commonplace on Ul'ianovskaia oblast city's trolley system. "Governor's Bread" also remained until the very end of the Goriachev administration. However, the administration sometimes failed to reimburse Ul'ianovskkhlebtorg, and the demand for the bread was such that the stores were often without it by mid-day.

28. According to the regional statistical agency, there were 1324 social organizations registered in the oblast in 1999. Ul'ianovskaia Oblast Committee for state Statistics, *Ekonomicheskoe polozhenie Ul'ianovskoi oblasti v 1999 godu* (Ul'ianovsk: Ul'ianovskaia Oblast Committee for State Statistics, 2000) 233.

29. Ema Grigoreevna, interview with author, tape recording, Ul'ianovsk, Ul'ianovskaia oblast,12 July 2001.

30. Elena Gavrilova, "Detskie posobiia tol'ko na bednost,'" *Simbirksii Kurer*, 11 March 2000.

31. Mikhail Zasypkin, interview with author, tape recording, Samara, Samarskaia oblast, 26 June 2001.

32. Political Section, "Bezproigryshnyi khod. Dazhe esli Moskva dob'etsia otmeny resheniia o pereschete v Samaraskoi oblasti pensii, Konstantin Titov ostanetsia v vyigryshe," *Samarskoe Obozrenie*, 22 November 1999.

33. Decree of the Governor of Samarskaia Oblast, "O merakh realizatsii federalnogo zakona 'O poriadke ischisleniia I uvelicheniia gosudarstvennykh pensii' na territorii Samarskoi oblasti," No. 290, 13 October 1999.

34. This partly accounts for the marked increase and restructuring of Samarskaia oblast's social service expenditures in 2000 (Table 2). Particularly, one should note the significant jump in the percentage of expenditures unaccounted for by the mandatory budget items.

35. Igor Valer'evich Averkiev, interview with author, Perm City, Perm, 22 June 2001. Regions like Perm had supplemented pensions in a more subtle way by using regional budget funds – the same procedure to which Titov subsequently resorted.

36. Dr. Evgenii Molevich, interview with author, Samara, Samarskaia oblast, 15 October 2000. See also, Zoia Andreeva, "Evgenii Molevich: Titov sam sozdal sebe oppozitsiiu," *Reporter*, 21 July 2000.

37. Fraser Mustard points to the importance of balancing primary wealth creation in what he refers to as the "real economy" with the provision of public goods like social services and health care. An emphasis on the latter may affect the former by resulting in under-investment and driving capital and other economic factors to other regions. The subsequent downturn in economic activity not only hurts the working sector of society, but also results in the eventual deterioration of public goods provision as tax revenues decline. On the other hand, under-investment in public goods provision creates a situation in which non-working sectors of society (pensioners, students, children, and invalids) are "excluded". See, Fraser Mustard, "Health, Health Care, and Social Cohesion" October 1998. 1 December 2001 <http://www.robarts.yorku.ca/pdf/apd_mustard.pdf>; R.G. Evans., "Health Care as a Threat to Health: Defense, Opulence, and the Social Environment", *Daedalus* 4 (1994) 2; R.G. Evans, and G.L. Stoddart, "Producing Health, Consuming Health Care", *Canadian Institute for the Advanced Research of Population Health Working Paper*, 6 (1990).

38. Titov won the 2000 regional executive election with 51% of the vote. Goriachev received only 24% of the regional vote and lost to his opponent.

39. The Ul'ianovskaia oblast study was an oblast-wide, 1630 respondent random survey undertaken in September of 2000 by the Ul'ianovsk State Technical University's "Perspektiv" Sociological Laboratory (Valentina Shuvalova, Director). The Samarskaia oblast survey was the third part of a four-stage survey of a 2099 respondent sample from the city of Samarskaia oblast, undertaken by the Samara Fund for Social Research in June 2000 (Vladimir Zvonovskii, Director).

40. The drop-off at the end of the 7th age category in the "Goriachev" curve results from the fact that the survey in Ul'ianovskaia oblast utilized seven age categories while the survey in Samarskaia oblast used eight. Nonetheless, the patterns of support are still indicative of the varying impact of the social policies on different age groups.

41. Assessments range from 1 "Poor" to 5 "Well off".

42. The categories were 1) incomplete elementary 2) complete elementary 3) elementary plus technical school 4) incomplete higher 5) complete higher.

43. Nonetheless, this study does not conclude with an endorsement for the indiscriminate application of the "Samarskaia oblast model" to other Russian regions. In many ways, Samarskaia oblast's reforms occurred in a rarified environment that would prove difficult to duplicate in many other regions. Somewhat ironically, Samarskaia oblast's liberal reforms were in part supported by the AvtoVAZ plant in Togliatti (a colossal "gift" of Soviet centralized planning), and the extensive gas pipelines and refineries occupy the region. AvtoVAZ produces nearly three-quarters of Russia's domestic automobiles and accounts for roughly 2% of all the taxes collected in the Russian Federation in 1999. While the firm is also a major tax holdout, the factory itself, along with the hundreds of local enterprises related to it, provides a large and relatively steady source of tax revenues for the oblast administration. Samarskaia oblast also enjoys natural resources in the form of oil and gas and substantial transport and refining infrastructure. Most members of the administration with whom I spoke indicated that these pre-existing factors contributed greatly to the oblast's success in restructuring the social and health sectors. Tax revenues played an especially important role in the social sector, both guaranteeing steady child welfare payments and allowing the governor to supplement pensions.

44. However, timing and preexisting resources are an important issue. Had the region continued to stagnate into both the 1996 and 2000 elections, Titov may have been unable to avoid the ire of a disadvantaged constituency. Furthermore, Samarskaia oblast's preexisting resource base also played a role in allowing the governor to pursue a more market-oriented strategy. Nonetheless, as argued above, Ul'ianovskaia oblast enjoyed similar advantages and the failure of its reform policies lends further support to the idea that policies and leadership matters.

THE TRANSFORMATIONS OF POSTCOMMUNIST WELFARE SYSTEMS: TRENDS AND POLICY LESSONS

MICHAEL J. G. CAIN

The issues associated with social welfare reforms in newly democratic states continue to be of vital interest to both international policy and research communities. For example policymakers tasked with analyzing possible threats to states, regions or the international system, have identified how reforms in social welfare systems can help strengthen weak states or prevent weak states from failing.* There is also a widely shared perspective among the donor community working in the Western Newly Independent States (NIS), the Caucuses and the Central Asian Republics on the need to assess what is known and what is not known about the restructuring of post-communist welfare states over the past 15 years. The research in this volume responds to these policy needs by sharing the research efforts of international experts on social welfare restructuring in post-communist states. Much of this research suggests that, when explaining patterns of social welfare reforms in post-communist countries, politics matter because the quality and type of welfare reforms are systematically related to the strength of democratic institutions and the mechanisms of accountability in a society.

This concluding chapter discusses the importance of research on social welfare reforms in transitioning states and points out general trends in post-communist welfare states following the collapse of state socialism in 1989. I then focus on attempts to explain these trends, drawing from the research presented in this volume. The essay ends with a discussion of particular policy lessons emerging from the conference.

---

* These social systems normally include institutions, policies and resources related to human capital investments for the maintenance and delivery of education and health care, social protection programs intended to assist poor or vulnerable populations such as disadvantaged youth, disabled heads of households or the elderly, as well as social insurances designed to reduce risks of unemployment, disability, sickness or old age occurring during adult life cycles.

SOCIAL WELFARE REFORMS IN OLD AND NEW DEMOCRACIES

Diverse welfare systems exist throughout Europe and Eurasia. Although there have been important advances in understanding how welfare states evolve, there remains a great deal to learn about the relationship of social welfare systems to economic and political development—not only in Central Europe and Eurasia but also throughout the developed world. Western research communities have yet to fully explain complex political and institutional linkages between citizens' desires for welfare protections, different income distributions and the provision of welfare by different types of government.[2] Papers presented in this volume by Anastassia Alexandrova and Polina Kuznetsova, Linda Cook, Johan DeDeken, Tomasz Inglot, Janelle Kerlin, Andrew Konitzer, Mitchell Orenstein, Dorottya Szikra, and Bela Tomka, shed new light on different aspects of these linkages over a broad range of transitioning states. Their findings illustrate the importance of domestic political arrangements and the contribution of institutional histories for understanding reform processes in post-communist states. Their analyses provide expert perspectives on welfare system reforms that are often unavailable to informed observers of comparative political processes and post-communist transformations.

The research perspectives provided in this volume emphasize the importance of domestic politics and domestic institutions in contributing to welfare reforms in Central Europe and post-Soviet states. Collectively the chapters call into question commonly held beliefs about social welfare systems. For example, policy makers often underestimate the importance of social welfare programs for national and regional development. Consider the following as an illustration of a popular intuition held by many policymakers: higher taxes and welfare transfers reduce productivity, which will inevitably harm the economy. What support is there for this intuition? Recent studies of the Organization for Economic Co-operation and Development (OECD) countries as well as studies of transitioning states do not provide very strong empirical support for the link between levels of social spending and negative GDP growth, nor do they show much evidence of convergence toward zero growth rates.[3] In fact, countries that spend comparatively more on redistributive social welfare programs—both in samples of OECD states and in samples of transitioning states—often economically outperform countries that spend less on social welfare. If we concentrate on transitioning states, countries that spend more on social welfare such as the Central European states, have also tended to institute greater democratic reforms than their counterparts in Southeast Europe, Western NIS or Central Asia, while enjoying higher GDP growth.[4] Considering the recent empirical record of transitioning states, there is nothing inconsistent between the initiation of deep social welfare reforms, increasing social spending and strengthening democracy and markets.

I do not want to suggest that increases in social spending and social transfers are always beneficial for economic growth and democratic development. Rather, I want to emphasize that basic empirical facts and intuitions associated with state welfare policies, economic output and democratic governance, remain poorly explained. Researchers contributing to this volume have spent many years looking at particular programs in state welfare systems, the evolution of these programs in transitioning societies and the political and institutional context of welfare reforms, in order that they might better understand how different social programs ultimately aid or hinder economic growth, how they impact poverty or inequality, as well as how welfare reforms promote or hinder civil society and democratic development. Their findings provide highly detailed examples of how different political, economic and social factors combine to produce successful or unsuccessful post-communist welfare policies and programs.

Why look at welfare state development in East Central Europe? The context of transitioning and newly-democratic states presents researchers with a historically unique laboratory in which to observe the evolution of new systems of welfare from similar—though by no means identical—starting points. Because of the homogenizing influence of communism on these societies, they share important legacies that reduce the set of possible causal antecedents that contribute to this diversity. The circumstances of post-socialist states offer important comparative possibilities for analyzing political and economic change that is vital for explaining different puzzles associated with the evolution of welfare states.

HOW MUCH REFORM AND HOW MUCH SOCIAL SPENDING?

The 28 post-communist states in Europe and Eurasia now exhibit enormous variation in economic productivity, political development, regime design and the organization and provision of social welfare. It is therefore impossible to fully describe all of the variations in social insurance and social protection programs in transitioning states over time. Perhaps because of the complexity of welfare states in transitioning societies, the papers in this volume illustrate a fundamental disagreement on the extent to which reforms have changed Central European welfare states over the last 15 years. Looking mainly at the transformation of pension systems in Central European states, Johan DeDeken argues that neoliberal pension models advocated by the World Bank and other Western agencies have taken root throughout much of Central Europe. By contrast, after comparing welfare programs in the Czech Republic, Hungary and Poland, Bela Tomka concludes that despite the importance of Western influences on transformation welfare states, "the liberal transformation of welfare systems has not taken place anywhere in East Central Europe".

Whatever one's view on the extent or types of reforms that have occurred in Central European countries since 1989, it is abundantly clear that different patterns of welfare expenditures have emerged among post-communist countries—patterns that produced very different social outcomes. In general, countries in East Central Europe, including the Czech Republic, Hungary, Poland, and Slovakia, spend comparatively more on social welfare than other post-communist countries, with a larger proportion of benefits going to poor households. Measured as a percent of GDP, public social spending in East Central European states has converged to European Union (EU) levels. For example, EU countries on average devote approximately 24 percent of GDP to social expenditures. The Czech Republic and Hungary spends 20.1 percent each, Poland 23 percent and Slovakia 17.9 percent.[5] By contrast, Russia and countries in Eurasia have spent considerably less on cash social transfers compared to their Central European counterparts, with much of the benefits going to non-poor households. Although precise estimates are difficult to find, the poorest of the Commonwealth of Independent States (CIS) spend somewhere between 3 percent (Armenia and Uzbekistan) and 6 percent (Azerbaijan and Moldova) of formal GDP on social protection.[6]

Besides differences in expenditure patterns, there are also important disparities in the distributional consequences of social spending. A growing body of research suggests that social spending in East Central European states has contributed to lower levels of inequality and poverty during the transition. Keane and Prasad argue that increased social spending in Poland mitigated inequality caused by wage disparities. Using household budget surveys from 1985-1997, they show that despite poor targeting of social cash transfers (including pensions), inequality and poverty was significantly reduced by these payments.[7] Using household survey data from the Czech Republic and Slovakia, Garner and Terrell reach similar results for the early transition period. Increases in inequality occurred because of changes in wage structure, but these changes were mitigated by adjustments in the tax and social transfer components in both republics.[8] Using household survey data for the early transition period in Bulgaria, Hassan and Peters show that the main social benefits, including pensions, offered in Bulgaria were pro-poor and therefore lessened inequality.[9] These recent household budget studies show that social welfare spending, though not well targeted to the poorest households, generally reduced inequality and poverty.

Central European countries spent considerably more on social welfare than Russia and NIS countries throughout the 1990s, resulting in reductions in poverty and inequality. Yet, because the circumstances in the Russian Federation and other Eurasian states are so different from Central Europe's, this fact is not as significant as it might seem. These countries, in many cases, have been unable to pay even the most basic social protection—old age pensions. Armenia, Georgia, Kyrgyzstan, Moldova, Russia, Tajikistan, Ukraine and Uzbekistan experienced varying degrees of pension arrears over various time periods. Using recent USAID data, Mitchell Orenstein's chapter shows that many pension systems in the CIS are inadequate to protect the poor from poverty, even when they do provide benefits. For example, Ukraine, Armenia, Azerbaijan and Moldova, provided less than $1.00 per day in average benefits. Even more alarming is the low coverage rate of pension systems in the CIS—dropping below 50 percent of the eligible, retired population. This suggests that pensions in the CIS will likely exacerbate income inequality in the near future, because only the most well off wage earners are covered by the systems currently in place.

Arrears combined with lower levels of social spending, poor targeting and inadequate pension capacity have been linked to higher levels of poverty. Klugman, Micklewright, and Redmond report that in Russia and Ukraine only 6 percent of social assistance spending went to the poorest fifth of the population.[10] Looking at all social spending programs in Russia from 1994 to 1998, Misikhina concludes that social benefits were regressive and that relatively wealthy families received a much larger fraction of benefits than poorer families.[11] Denisova, Kolenikov, and Yudaeva find that by 1996 only 33 percent of eligible families received child benefits.[12] Using household survey data, Grogan shows that from 1994 to 2000, there was no relationship between income level and the propensity to receive social benefits.[13] Instead, the likelihood of receiving child benefits in Russia was due to where you lived or when you applied for benefits—not whether your household qualified for child benefits.

When we combine recent household spending studies of transitioning countries, together they provide strong evidence that higher levels of social spending lessened inequality and poverty in East Central European states. They also show that lower levels of social spending and incomplete or inadequate restructuring of welfare institutions were linked to increasing inequality and higher levels of poverty in Russia and other countries of Eurasia. Viewed collectively, these studies suggest that spending levels in Central European welfare systems, combined with greater institutional capacity and increased reforms, may have been crucial factors for preventing even higher levels of poverty and inequality to emerge during transition.

WHAT EXPLAINS PATTERNS OF WELFARE STATE EXPENDITURES AND REFORM?

The chapters in this volume discuss a wide range of factors that explain changes in the design, organization and delivery of social welfare benefits in transitioning states. These factors include the characteristics inherited from communist societies and their welfare institutions, the influence of international agencies on welfare policies and the politics of welfare transformation in post-communist societies. However it is this last factor, the role of politics in the transformation of post-communist welfare states, which emerges as a key point of agreement among many contributors to this volume. This agreement on the importance of politics in welfare reform does not mean that economic considerations played no role; after the first stage of transition when deep recessions were gradually abating, Central European states faced pressures to retrench their 'reformed' welfare states by controlling public expenditures and by reducing or eliminating a wide range of social benefits. States also needed to introduce administrative policy reforms to achieve what Linda Cook calls "market-conforming" welfare systems, to adapt features of these systems originally intended to support socialist economies. Economic influences were always a common factor in reforms across all post-communist welfare systems.

But it seems that politics matter in ways that are unique to the region, especially when compared with Western welfare state development. Politics matter both in terms of what was missing in post-communist societies, for example the weakness of civil society, and in terms of how strong democratic governance took root in a given country. Unlike the transformation and development of welfare systems in Western states, the role of organized, class-based interests demanding specific types of welfare protections never emerged in Central Europe. Bela Tomka suggests this was related to the organizational disadvantages among welfare recipients and their inability to organize interests into a more potent political force. However the inability of groups to organize was also related to the poverty of social capital inherent in post-communist civil societies. In her chapter, Linda Cook generally agrees with this view, arguing that the main recipients of social welfare benefits in Central Europe had considerably less influence on policy outcomes than Western counterparts. This occurred because of weaknesses associated with developing representative organizations and weaknesses in newly formed democratic institutions responsible for expressing these interests. Johan DeDeken suggests that trade unions that might have represented the welfare interest of the population in post-communist states were often weak agents of change and subject to the risk of being too closely associated with discredited communist regimes. Contributors to this volume appear to agree that communist legacies associated with weak civil society and limitations in nascent democratic institutions probably combined to limit the voice of crucial interests throughout the period of transformation in post-communist welfare states.

In spite of the weakness of civil society and the inadequate links between interests and representative institutions, authors in this volume also agree that the quality and character of democratic governance play a key role in explaining divergent patterns in social welfare policies and outcomes. The papers presented here provide a variety of evidence pointing to the importance of democratization in successful transformations in the welfare state. Unlike the CIS, Central European social welfare reforms were implemented in a more gradual manner, involving greater numbers of social actors, greater consultation and frequently greater contestation between political and civil society coalitions. This often resulted in negotiated welfare reforms in many Central European states.

By contrast, reforms in the CIS were often carried out without democratic accountability. Instead, executives were free to cut expenditures and social benefits, change or reform pension or social systems unconstrained by interest groups or even statist elements of social bureaucracies. Johan DeDeken forcefully argues that the less a country has democratized the better able it is at adhering to some ideal orthodoxy in welfare state practices—whether an old Soviet orthodoxy in Belarus or a neoliberal pension orthodoxy advocated by Western actors in Kazakhstan. Moreover, as Andrew Konitzer and Anastassia Alexandrova and Polina Kuznetsova show, weak governance in Russia resulted in poor social welfare planning, botched implementation and often incoherent welfare reform policies. In short, strengthening democracy and governance likely increases the ability of the state to plan and implement social policies, while making it more likely that reforms are closer to the general wishes of the electorate.

Many international agencies have attempted to strengthen local democracy and governance in post-communist states by advocating the decentralization of social welfare services and benefits. However a wide range of unanticipated problems emerged from these recommendations. As Janelle Kerlin notes in her study of decentralized social service reforms in Poland, recommendations from international agencies emboldened central administrators to rapidly devolve responsibilities to local governments without providing the fiscal authority necessary to meet these new responsibilities. In the end many social programs were never implemented due to insufficient funding. Alexandrova and Kuznetsova found similar problems emerging in Russia's oblasts. The attempt at the federal level to monetize social benefits in Russia occurred largely without input from regional authorities. The result was only modest success in rationalizing the system of social benefits in regional governments. Whether attempting reforms in Central Europe or Eurasia, it appears that the process of reform strongly influences the quality of reform outcomes. Politics indeed matter in almost any type of reform process.

What lessons can we learn from the new democracies of Central Europe?

Johan DeDeken's critical essay reminds us that drawing policy lessons from another country's experience can be very difficult, even when these lessons are drawn from a country with similar histories and experiences. Given this caveat, there are several important policy recommendations that emerge from these essays, which may help guide policymakers in developing recommendations for improvements in social protections and social benefits in post–Soviet states. Among the many policy suggestions that appear in these essays, allow me to point out those that emerge from an agreement between two or more contributors to this volume:

- Better, more transparent democratic processes linked with increased government capacity will contribute to improved social policy processes that reinforce rather than weaken social welfare reforms.
- Strong executives, unconstrained by other state actors and without mechanisms of civic accountability, often produce low quality policy changes that can have significant negative side effects for the provision of social welfare.
- Transparency in national-level policymaking can help prevent exclusionary policymakers from capturing and controlling key elements of reform policy.
- Frequent reforms to social benefit systems or recurrent policy changes can diminish the poverty protection qualities of social systems by introducing unpredictability and uncertainty in eligibility and benefit provision.
- Because the administration of mandatory, private pension systems are complex and require strong regulatory capacities, weak states should opt for simple pension systems that provide high coverage at low costs.
- Changes in national social welfare policies should always consider the impacts of policy changes on national public expenditures and local government finances.

- The decentralization of social services and benefits work best when it occurs within a broader national plan of decentralization of fiscal authority.
- The decentralization of social services and benefits in weak states often lead to a reduction in benefits to the poor or a decrease in social benefits.
- National governments should pay attention to factors that affect regional policy making, since knowledge of these factors can help predict success or failure in national reforms.

These policy lessons by no means exhaust the detailed suggestions that appear in many papers in this volume. Nevertheless, they provide general policy prescriptions from almost fifteen years of post-communist experience in social welfare transformation. As Tomasz Inglot points out, besides these policy lessons, there are important scholarly themes that emerge from the chapters in this volume that have very practical implications for policymakers.

ENDNOTES

1. Department of International Development (DFID), "Why We Need to Work More Effectively in Fragile States," London: (January, 2005). United Nations Development Program (UNDP), "The Inflexibility Trap: Frustrated Societies, Weak States and Democracy," Brastislava: (August, 2002). United States Agency for International Development (USAID), "Fragile State Strategy," Washington D.C.: (2005).

2. Alberto Alesina, Edward Glaeser, and Bruce Sacerdote, "Why Doesn't the United States Have a European-Style Welfare State?" *Brookings Paper on Economic Activity*, 2. (2001). Charles Boix, *Democracy and Redistribution*, (Cambridge: Cambridge University Press, 2003). Torben Iverson and David Soskice, "Electoral Institutions, Parties, and the Politics of Class: How Come Democracies Redistribute More Than Others," (April, 2005). Karl Ove Moene and Michael Wallerstein, "Inequality, Social Insurance and Redistribution," *American Political Science Review* 95:4 (2001): 859-874.

3. Peter H. Lindert, *Growing Public: Social Spending and Economic Growth Since the Eighteenth Century*, (Cambridge: Cambridge University Press, 2004). William Easterly, William G. Gale, and Joel Slemrod, "What Do Cross-Country Studies Teach About Government Involvement, Prosperity, and Economic Growth?" *Brookings Paper on Economic Activity*, 2, (1995): 373-431.

4. Michael P. Keane and Eswar S. Prasad, "Inequality, Transfers, and Growth: New Evidence from the Economic Transition in Poland," *International Monetary Fund Working Paper*, (June 2000).

5. Förster and Mira D'Ercole , "Income distribution and poverty in OECD countries in the second half of the 1990s", *OECD Social, Employment and Migration Working Papers*, forthcoming, OECD, (Paris, 2005).

6. Anton Dobronogov, "Social Protection in Low Income CIS Countries," (Prepared for the Lucerne Conference of the CIS-7 Initiative), (January 2003).

7. Michael P. Keane and Eswar S. Prasad, "Changes in the Structure of Earnings During the Polish Transition," *International Monetary Fund Working Paper*, (August 2002).

8. T.I. Garner and K. Terrell, "A Gini Decomposition Analysis of Inequality in the Czech and Slovak Republics During the Transition," *Economics of Transition*, 6:1 (1996): 23-46.

9. F.M.A. Hassan and R.K. Peters, Jr. "The Structure of Incomes and Social Protection During the Transition: The Case of Bulgaria," *Europe-Asia Studies*, 48:4 (1996): 629-646.

10. Jeni Klugman, John Micklewright, and Gerry Redmond, "Fighting Poverty in the Transition: Social Expenditures and the Working-Age Poor," UNICEF Innocenti Research Centre, Florence (2001).

11. S. Misikhina, "Social Benefits and Subsides in the Russian Federation" Technical Aid to the Commonwealth States (TACIS)/ European Union (EU, (1999).

12. I. Denisova, S. Kolenikov, and K. Yudaev, "Child Benefits and Child Poverty," (Unpublished Manuscript), (2000).

13. L. Grogan, "Social Transfers and Intra-household Resource Allocation: Evidence from Russia," (Guelph, Canada: University of Guelph Press: 2004).